The One Question You Nee
without Gimmicks, Hyp

CW01510533

Simple
Marketing
—— *for* ——
Smart
People

BILLY BROAS
with TIAGO FORTE

For Kuki

Contents

Foreword

ALI ABDAAL

I'll never forget that fateful day a few months after I'd traded my stethoscope for a MacBook and a YouTube channel. It was the launch day of my first online course. The room was tense; my finger hovered over the publish button, a gateway to a new phase of my life. If twelve people bought this course, I would consider it a win, a sign that my pivot away from working full time as a doctor wasn't an utter delusion. I took a deep breath, clicked, and waited.

Refresh. 125 customers. $50,000 in revenue.

Refresh again. $65,000.

Another refresh. $85,000.

Within minutes, the numbers spiraled up to $150,000. This was more money than I had ever seen in my life—a full-time doctor working sixty-hour weeks in the UK's National Health Service could work three years to earn that sum. And here I was, in utter disbelief, having made it in three minutes.

By the end of launch week, we'd hit $350,000, and it was crystal clear: my life had changed forever.

I mention this because just a few weeks before this whirlwind, I was what you might call a "marketing noob."

Marketing, and especially sales, felt like dirty words to me. I thought marketing was about billboards and slimy infomercials, and sales was the thing someone selling used cars did with body odor and false promises to lure you in.

But as I was transitioning out of my full-time job as a doctor, I knew my business needed a stream of revenue that wasn't dependent on YouTube ads and sponsorships. I wanted to sell my own product, something I built myself that I could sell to my audience. And because I was familiar with educational content, I thought an online course would make sense. Perhaps an online course where I could teach people what I'd learned about growing a YouTube channel over the past three years?

I knew I could create the course. But selling it—that was a whole other ball game. It was going to be my first digital product, and I didn't want it to come across as scammy, with countdown timers, HUGE TEXT, and bright colors flashing in your face.

Around that time, I enrolled in Tiago Forte's course, *Building a Second Brain*. I loved the course and especially loved Tiago's approach to selling it. Even though I'd paid thousands of dollars for the course, I never felt "sold to," or coerced into buying it. There was something seriously classy about Tiago's operation. And I knew the course was generating millions in revenue.

So I reached out to him, asking for advice about how to sell my own course, hoping for even a fraction of the secret sauce Tiago seemed to have. Tiago very kindly shared his whole method and connected me with the genius behind his own marketing: a gentleman named Billy Broas.

And that was how, a few weeks before launching my first online course, I started working with Billy to learn how marketing actually works, how it isn't about shiny objects, countdown timers, and scammy-looking sales pages, how it isn't about manipulation—it's about education.

The lessons and strategies I learned from Billy were what I directly applied to my own business to make six figures with our very first launch.

The principles he taught me have been central to our sales and marketing ever since. Three years since that first launch, we now make several million dollars a year in profit directly from selling courses online. In fact, as I write this, we've just run a Black Friday promotion (using Billy's Belief Building approach that you will learn in this book).

While I've been on a diving and yoga retreat in Mexico, my team has run a series of email campaigns that have driven over $500,000 in revenue over the past four days, with zero involvement from me. I know—it's completely wild.

I share all of this because I resonate deeply with the readers this book aims to serve—the smart, academic, non-marketers who find themselves in a jungle of complexity and shiny objects. The people who, like me, were scared of sales and marketing and of coming across as slimy sleazeballs. Had I not learned what this book teaches—had I not met Billy and Tiago—I might still be pressing refresh, waiting for the first dozen customers.

Thanks to Billy's help, I now know the profound importance of understanding your customer, crafting a meaningful offer, and thoughtfully addressing objections. I appreciate the value of focusing on my core message and how the platform-specific tactics are the cherry on top rather than the cake itself. And I no longer think of marketing as the thing you think about after you've created your product, but rather, a core part of creating your product in the first place.

Simple Marketing for Smart People is the marketing playbook you didn't know you needed. It's a thoughtful, educational approach to marketing that demystifies the complex and often misunderstood world of selling your ideas, products, or services. This book isn't about shortcuts or tricks; it's about building a solid foundation in understanding how to communicate your value effectively and authentically.

As you turn these pages, you'll discover that marketing, at its core, is about clarity and connection. It's about understanding the people you wish to serve and crafting your message to resonate with them deeply. Billy and Tiago can break down complex marketing concepts into digestible, actionable steps that anyone can follow.

Billy's approach is refreshing in a world where marketing advice often feels overhyped or disconnected from reality. It shows that you don't need to compromise your integrity or values to market effectively. Instead, Billy advocates for a marketing style rooted in teaching, sharing, and genuinely helping your audience.

In *Simple Marketing for Smart People*, you'll find a road map to marketing success that aligns with your intelligence and integrity. It's the guide I wish I had when I started my journey as an entrepreneur, and it's the guide I'm thrilled to recommend to anyone looking to navigate the complexities of marketing in today's world.

Embrace these lessons, and you'll not just sell more products or services— you'll build trust, authority, and lasting relationships with your audience. And perhaps, like me, you'll find yourself looking back on your marketing journey, amazed at how far you've come, and excited about the opportunities that lie ahead.

Happy reading!
Ali Abdaal

Introduction

There was a time when complexity almost killed me—literally.

My name is Billy Broas, and in my early twenties, I worked for an engineering company specializing in clean energy. In my off time, I became a home beer brewer to scratch a creative itch. If you've met a home brewer, you know we enjoy building our brewery almost as much as we enjoy making beer.

After several years of indulging in my hobby, I found myself wanting to upgrade my brewing setup to something bigger and better. I searched Google and finally landed on my dream brewery. A former NASA scientist had designed it and published his blueprints online.

His brewery was the most beautiful thing I'd ever laid eyes on.

It was also complex as heck. At no small expense, I undertook a massive twelve-month project to build this "space age" brewing rig. After I tightened that final bolt, I took a step back and gazed upon my creation. All my dreams seemed fulfilled.

Three stainless steel pots rested atop their propane burners. Rows of buttons dotted the control panel. Pipes connected to more pipes, which connected to hoses. Two heavy-duty pumps powered the entire system.

My home brewery was badass.

But, the more time I spent with it, the more I saw its fatal flaw. It had way too many moving parts and constantly malfunctioned. Pipes leaked, burners failed, and hoses clogged. I spent more time fixing that darn setup than doing what I intended to do: brew great beer.

One Sunday afternoon, I was deep in the trenches with the malfunctions. A gasket burst, leaving me soaking wet and pretty pissed off. I stormed off my patio where the brewery lived and walked into my kitchen.

In my rush, I accidentally hung a towel on the edge of the brewing equipment—right next to a propane burner.

Just as I shut the kitchen door, an automatic timer hit zero and clicked on the burner. Its blue flame leaped into action.

Preoccupied with the gadget I was cleaning in the kitchen sink, I first noticed the fire out of the corner of my eye. My head whipped around to the window where I saw the terrifying scene: the towel I'd hung on the brewery had burst into flames right next to my house.

I ran outside, grabbed a mop, used its wooden handle to fling the blazing inferno into a bucket of cold water, and watched the flames die down to a flicker. Thank God.

If I had waited one more minute, the fire would have spread to the propane tank, which could have exploded and blown up my home—and possibly me. Needless to say, that was the *last* time I indulged in the messy and dangerous affair of my complicated NASA brewery.

What I didn't realize was how this story would one day parallel my experience in marketing.

If you are reading this, my guess is you picked up this book because you want to market your product or service, and you are probably tired of your attempts backfiring. You may have come close to blowing up your business more than once because of a faulty investment, or felt defeated by the amount of time you spent marketing with little return.

You aren't alone. I've seen many smart people attempt marketing only to watch their best efforts go up in flames.

The big problem is this: many well-intended business owners are building an online marketing presence that too closely resembles my NASA brewery. They're drowning in social media platforms, website plugins, landing pages, email marketing, AI, and dozens of other bells and whistles.

Just as my overly complicated brewery robbed my attention from what mattered most—the beer—all this marketing complexity can too easily rob your attention from what matters most: your core marketing message.

Who You Are

If you're like Tiago (my co-author) and me, then growing up you weren't one of those kids people called a natural-born entrepreneur. Tiago and I sure weren't—we were nerds.

In fifth grade, I would finish my quizzes early and sit next to my teacher, and we would read our *Popular Science* magazines together. Our favorite part was the What's New section, which featured all the latest inventions and technology.

I thrived in school, received a BS in integrated science and technology, and eventually received my MBA.

Not once along this journey did I attempt an entrepreneurial endeavor. Sure, I'd dream about developing inventions and business ventures, but those ideas stayed in my head—I never acted upon them.

When I finally did reach the point where I wanted to start my own business, I realized I needed skills I hadn't been taught in school. I needed the skills possessed by people like Gary.

Gary Vaynerchuk was eight years older than me and lived in a nearby New Jersey suburb. When he was seven, Gary started a lemonade stand franchise. When he was a teenager, he'd sell baseball cards at his local shopping mall on the weekends. After graduating college, Gary took over his dad's wine store and grew it to millions of dollars in revenue.

While I've never met my fellow New Jerseyan, I have massive respect for Gary. Gary calls himself a "purebred entrepreneur."[1]

If you've picked up this book, I'm guessing you're more like me than Gary, more of an academic than a natural-born salesperson. And I'm guessing, like me, you wish you had some of his skill with selling.

But here's what I've learned: even if we aren't purebred entrepreneurs, we can still be successful in business for ourselves.

You've learned a skill, created a valuable product or service, and are getting results for your customers. You've said, "Wow, maybe I'm an entrepreneur after all."

Now you want to get to the next level, and you're asking the question we've all asked: "How do I reach more customers?"

Dread hits your stomach as you arrive at your answer. "I have to do marketing."

You've come to the right place.

You likely have an aversion to marketing, but we can assure you this book's approach isn't based on gimmicks or hype, but on timeless principles, classical techniques, and deep empathy for customers.

---

1   I first discovered Gary through his video podcast, "Wine Library TV." This was in 2007. I came across him because people in the craft beer world were talking about him, and with my homebrewing website, I was deeply entrenched in the beer industry. You can find him at https://tv.winelibrary.com/.

Instead of being loud, we teach a more nuanced way to communicate your product's value. It's a more academic approach that still allows for storytelling, creativity, and of course—excellent financial success.

This book's approach is technology agnostic and medium agnostic, meaning you can use it across any social media site or email software, and whether you're creating text, audio, or video.

Finally, this book's approach is simple—it doesn't have many moving parts. As I learned with my brewery, the best solutions are simple and elegant. At the heart of this book is one simple question that streamlines your marketing efforts.

But simple does not mean easy. Marketing is difficult—there's no way around it. Creating profitable marketing is recognized as one of the business world's most challenging endeavors. That doesn't mean marketing must be complicated or confusing, however. It can, indeed, be simple.

Billy

Again, my name is Billy Broas, and I've partnered with my client, business partner, and now friend, Tiago Forte, to write the marketing book we wish we'd had when we first struck out on our own.

I sold my first product online in 2010. At the time of publishing, I've been the behind-the-scenes strategist for twenty-nine entrepreneurs, launched seventy-five marketing campaigns, and have generated over $20 million in organically driven revenue (i.e., without paid advertising). For many of my clients, I've doubled or tripled their yearly revenue. In addition to working directly with businesses, I've coached 165 people in my group programs, and 500 more have enrolled in my online courses.

The feedback I hear most from clients is that I help them achieve growth that lasts—not just temporary spikes. This book embodies that philosophy, providing you with strategies for sustainable growth in a noisy world.

I used to believe that to win at marketing, I had to be the loudest. I used to believe that it was only the extroverted, natural-born entrepreneurs who made sales—while we more reserved people were ignored.

Now I know it's possible to sell my products and services by being myself. In fact, I know that our best shot at success comes from being ourselves.

But yes, our modern world is noisy. Each day, the people you want as your customers are bombarded with ads, articles, videos, and online content from companies fighting for their attention.

How can you cut through that noise?

You must meet your customers where they are and walk the journey with them to buying your product. There's no skipping this step—it's your only shot.

Now, meet my co-author, Tiago Forte.

Tiago

Hi, I'm Tiago Forte. I'm a productivity coach who started out in business to help people get organized and accomplish more. My main product is an online course called *Building a Second Brain,* and I have a book by the same name.

Billy asked me to help him write this book because (as Billy explained to me) my story exemplifies the smart person's struggles when it comes to marketing.

I knew exactly what he meant. Billy's teachings about marketing have had a hugely positive impact on me, so I told him yes.

It's true—I was once in your position, looking to finally crack the code on selling my products and services. In fact, I still wrestle with it.

Although my products have been successful by most standards, getting them to that point was by no means easy. Like any online business owner, I struggled with shiny objects, self-doubt, and marketing overwhelm.

In this book, I want to share with you the most important lessons Billy taught me about marketing, and how I've used them in my business. It's changed the way I approach not just marketing, but product creation and communication as a whole.

After you learn Billy's strategies, especially his concept of Belief Building, you'll look at marketing through a new lens and you will be so much better off for it.

Okay, I (Billy) am back. Let's jump into the book.

Here's our path:

In **Chapter One**, you'll learn why the curse of knowledge throws a wrench into smart people's marketing efforts and how to redirect your brainpower to where it matters most in marketing.

In **Chapter Two,** you'll hear Tiago's story of growing his online business and his three big "smart person" mistakes.

Chapter Three introduces our guiding metaphor that explains what marketing really is. (Hint: it's not your website.)

Chapter Four teaches you the one question you need to ask to simplify all your marketing efforts—a technique inherited from history's great copywriters.

Chapter Five shares Tiago's experience using Belief Building in marketing his products, including a belief that almost caused a customer revolt.

Chapter Six gives you three methods to help you discover your prospect's current beliefs, which you'll need in order to walk the buying journey with them.

Chapter Seven gives you the steps to identify the beliefs your customer needs to value your offerings properly.

Chapter Eight enters the content creation phase of Belief Building. No more throwing spaghetti at the wall when it comes to creating marketing content. It's time to get strategic.

Chapter Nine shows you how to build trust with everything you publish and win over even your most skeptical prospects.

Chapter Ten shows you our entire process from start to finish by creating three pieces of marketing content for Tiago's online course. You'll love the real-world example.

Chapter Eleven reveals how our approach is a hidden pattern you'll start to see out in the world and for any type of product, from accounting software to grocery store food.

Chapter Twelve gives you smart next steps for implementing our *Simple Marketing for Smart People* approach, so you can see immediate results with your current and prospective clients and customers.

In the conclusion, you'll hear an inspiring story that demonstrates why it's so important for you to market yourself.

There you go—a simple marketing approach for smart people.

If you're ready to reframe your view on marketing, to see it as something other than manipulation, deception, flashy websites, and fifteen-second viral videos, and if you're excited about the idea that marketing can be human-first, education-driven, creative, fun, and yes, *profitable*—this is the book for you.

Let's dive into Chapter One and discover **why even the brightest people struggle with marketing**.

Grab These Free Resources
To Implement This Book's Approach

Don't just read this book—put it into action! You'll find implementation easier with these free resources. Go to this book's bonus page and get:

1. A cheat sheet for the book's key concepts.
2. A template for your core messaging document.
3. Real-life examples of marketing material that follows the *Simple Marketing for Smart People* approach.

Head to SimpleMarketingBook.com/bonus
to get these free resources, or scan the QR code below:

CHAPTER ONE

The Achilles' Heel of Smart People

By BILLY BROAS

In the James Bond films, there's a recurring scene fans have come to anticipate. At the end of each movie, the criminal mastermind, despite his intellect, always falls into the trap of overcomplication.

Once he finally captures James Bond, the criminal decides to eliminate Bond using an overly elaborate scheme. Bond, of course, escapes and prevails.

A classic example is in the film *Live and Let Die*, where the villain decides to kill Bond by handcuffing him to a platform and then slowly lowering the platform into a shark-infested tank. Bond has plenty of time to free himself from the handcuffs, take out the villain, and get the girl.[1]

This classic spy film trope was later mocked in Mike Myers's 1997 movie, *Austin Powers: International Man of Mystery*, so it's clearly hitting on something real.[2]

This archetypal movie scene portrays the double-edged sword of smart people: they have a sharp mind, but it often backfires.

Their smart mind is wonderful and brings them many benefits. But that same mind also causes them to constantly overthink and overcomplicate.

---

1   Guy Hamilton director, *Live and Let Die*, (1973; London, United Kingdom: Eon Productions).
2   Mike Myers, *Austin Powers: International Man of Mystery*, Jay Roach director, (1997; Santa Clarita, CA: Capella International).

I overcomplicated my home brewery like crazy.

When I read the NASA scientist's blueprints, I became excited. Blinded by my enthusiasm to build this technologically advanced brewery, I never stopped and asked if this is even the best way to brew beer.

After nearly blowing myself up and accepting defeat with my NASA brewery, I tried a different approach.

The next time I brewed, I did the opposite of my usual, complex method. I made things simple.

I walked into my pantry and grabbed my spaghetti pot. You've seen those big metal pots with handles on the sides. That's all I really needed. With this simple setup, I had no pipes or valves or blinking screens.

I could get closer to what really matters in brewing: the core ingredients. I finally had the time to *taste* the beer at each step during the process, ensuring the flavor was on track.

I popped coffee-flavored grains into my mouth, contrasting them with the chocolate grains. I had time to smell the aroma rising from the green hop flowers, noticing the subtle differences between varieties, one like grapefruit, the other lemon.

I was more like a chef, less like an engineer.

In cooking and in brewing, tasting your creation along the way and choosing the appropriate ingredients allows you to make the upstream decisions that have the biggest downstream impact on the beer's final flavor.

Upstream decisions are vital because they occur earlier in a process and thus lock in your direction. If you choose the wrong direction, each move you make in that (wrong) direction—skilled as that move may be—will have limited impact.

Brewing is a long process, often taking months for the beer to be ready to drink, so the decisions you make upstream are far more important than those downstream. If you make a mistake on the day you brew the batch, that mistake will become locked in and difficult to fix after the beer's been fermenting for three months.

Avoiding upstream mistakes is crucial in both brewing and marketing. Good upstream decisions can often compensate for downstream errors.

For example, I once filled fifty bottles of beer, only to realize later that one bottle hadn't been cleaned properly. That one bottle spoiled, but I still had forty-nine good bottles. Downstream mistakes tend to have a less significant impact on the overall outcome.

They don't have as large an impact on your overall results.

The tricky thing about upstream mistakes is that they're easy to make, especially when you're distracted. With my NASA brewery, all those bells and whistles distracted me from the upstream decisions that made the biggest positive impact, like choosing the appropriate ingredients for that batch of beer.

My day one mistakes became locked in and there was no hope of fixing those on day two, let alone day ninety.

The lesson is clear: when you keep things simple, you free up the time, attention, and headspace to invest in what matters most.

(And in most cases, going back to simple will also free up cash.)

We'll go further into this upstream/downstream metaphor in Chapter Three. Once you learn how it applies to marketing, you'll see marketing as much more doable.

Now, I wish I could tell you the near-explosion of my brewery taught me this "don't overcomplicate" lesson once and for all, but it didn't. I learned it again when I started my first online business.

After getting good at brewing beer, I decided to turn my hobby into a business. Not by selling beer, but rather, by teaching others how to make it. I launched a website and decided to sell courses training people how to brew beer at home.

In the early days, my beer brewing website was a side hustle. I'd work on the website in the evenings after coming home from my day job. I enjoyed my job and was in no big rush to leave, but I knew the day would eventually come when I'd want to be free, so in order to be financially ready for that day, I needed to sell more online courses—a task I found much more difficult than expected.

Similar to how I taught myself beer brewing, I decided to teach myself marketing. Educating myself had always been my solution to any problem, so why should this part of running a business be any different?

Being a curious and analytical person, I had to read and understand every marketing article I found. The problem was the flow of articles never stopped. As I tore through those articles, telling myself it was a good use of my time because I was learning, I kept delaying progress in my online business. Those delays made it more unlikely I'd ever be able to leave the world of the nine to five.

I quickly learned with marketing that it's easy for the never-ending stream of information to do more harm than good. I had a stack of possible tactics but no clear place to start. I kept learning instead of implementing, and this led to feelings of guilt and frustration.

I was good at homebrewing and could teach it to anyone, but nobody knew that because they didn't know about me or my online courses.

My story is all too common.

Why Do Smart People Overcomplicate?

To begin, we have to ask why *do* smart people overcomplicate things?

One reason: because you're able to.

You have a sharp mind, and you know how to use it. It's served you well, too. It's helped you thrive in your profession. You understand your topic better than 99% of people.

You're also detail-oriented and notice nuances others miss.

When it comes to your topic, do you often see distinctions others don't?

When my buddy walks up to the bartender and says, "I'll have a beer," my brain spins.

"What is he talking about?!"

"Does he mean an IPA? A stout? A pilsner?"

Given all I've learned about beer making, my brain has turned one category (beer) into hundreds of categories (the 150+ styles of beer).

Who knew ordering a beer could be so complicated?

Here's my point: when you have an analytical mind and dive deep into a topic, one topic becomes many. It splits into hundreds or thousands of subtopics.

Do you now see why smart people are prone to getting lost in details?

When experts talk about "being in the weeds," this is what they mean. Those details are the weeds, and those weeds are tough to escape.

Most of the time, getting into the weeds benefits you. You're able to see distinctions and find better solutions. But when it comes time to market those solutions? Be careful.

The mindset you had down in the weeds is not the same mindset you want to bring to the marketplace. You'll confuse people with your technical talk. The Belief Building approach we share in this book will help you find the right words.

The other risk when you study marketing is that you are likely to confuse *yourself*.

Marketing is incredibly broad and deep. You also have to deal with a constantly changing landscape of regulatory, legal, and societal issues. Not to mention you're constantly bombarded by a growing list of platforms, technologies, and tools.

It's overwhelming.

The smart person runs the risk of approaching marketing the way they approach any topic—diving into the details and thinking they need to learn every tool or channel to become successful.

But running headfirst into marketing isn't the key to mastering it. You're too likely to get lost. Rather than aim for an exhaustive understanding, focus on the critical parts. Believe it or not, your brain is well suited to mastering marketing—you simply need to focus your brain on the right target.

"Can't I Just Outsource My Marketing?"

I know what you're thinking: Can't I just outsource or delegate my marketing?

Nobody can blame you. Heck, we've all asked that question.

And it's reasonable because, after all, you've put all that time and energy into learning your topic, and other people have put the time into learning marketing, so why not hire *them*?

On paper, outsourcing your marketing makes sense. In my experience, it never turns out well.

Oh, you can outsource marketing *activities*. You can hire an agency to create Facebook ads, do graphic design, and maybe even write emails for you.

But who creates the core message that the agency uses? And how is that twenty-year-old intern supposed to know the language of a topic you've been immersed in for decades? How much empathy can you expect that employee to have for your future customers?

And here's another good question: Can the person you hire for marketing recognize when someone *isn't* a good fit for your business?

You can see where this is going.

This is why you must make these decisions internally—not outsource them. Even a giant corporation like the Coca-Cola Company, which uses multiple ad agencies, has an internal marketing department.

Nobody understands your business like you do.

Marketing isn't just an activity or a department. You weave marketing into everything your business communicates, from your products to your mission statement to your newsletter emails. And if you attempt to isolate or delegate this communication, it will not be as strong or as cohesive as it needs to be. Not if you want to compete in today's noisy world.

Business is hard enough. Don't make it harder by bringing a muddy marketing message to the table.

Again, go nuts with outsourcing marketing activities, like hiring someone to create your website or post to your Facebook page. Chapter Three will give you many ideas on what you can outsource in your marketing.

But your core marketing message? That must be created by you.

Don't worry, we've got you covered.

CHAPTER TWO

I Can Relate

By TIAGO FORTE

I can relate to your struggles with marketing.

Like Billy, I've got my own distressing tale of overwhelm.

In 2007, I started feeling tension and a slight tickle at the back of my throat. What began as a tickle slowly over months and then years became an almost unbearable pain. I did every test and scan and diagnostic you can imagine, but the doctors could never find the root cause.

Finally, after years of suffering, a neurologist gave me a last resort. It was a powerful anti-seizure medication normally used to treat schizophrenia. The side effect was severe short-term memory loss. The drug eliminated my pain, but it also zapped my memory.

Books I read, meaningful conversations I had, and trips I took were gone as if they had never happened. I remember one day when I was serving in the Peace Corps in eastern Ukraine. I turned to my friend and fellow volunteer and said, "We should go visit Russia!" She turned to me in shock and said, "Tiago, we visited Moscow just a few months ago. Don't you remember?"

I didn't remember anything. Seeing the photos we had taken, which proved that I was there, felt vaguely familiar, but it was like looking at someone else's memories, of someone else's life.

I remember walking up to my doctor's receptionist one day and asking her for my complete patient record, which at that point was a huge stack of papers. I thought, "I need to understand this."

I took that stack of medical records and scanned each page one by one into my computer. I called the digital repository I was creating my "Second Brain" because I could no longer remember things with my first brain (i.e. my actual brain).

Now, think about your own life for a second. There is far too much information we have to remember, keep track of, and act on.

Too many details, too many facts, too much research, too many emails, too many to-dos, too many messages, too many things coming at us from all sides. In a way, my mysterious health condition gave me a window into a future in which our brains simply cannot keep up. It's not a question of whether you are productive enough or have the right computer setup. It's reaching a biological breaking point.

We've been hearing about information overload for over twenty years now. I constantly hear from my students, my customers, and my clients about the indecision, distraction, stress, anxiety, and procrastination they face. I think those symptoms have a common cause: the volume of information we have to deal with has become inhuman. It has far exceeded our capacity as human beings to manage.

One great solution is digital note-taking apps. I created my digital Second Brain to store the important information I wanted to remember: book notes, ideas from podcasts, quotes, work research, writing projects, and more.

What started as a personal quest to preserve the information that mattered to me, eventually became a thriving business that teaches people around the world how to do the same.

Even though I now run a successful business, I did not have previous experience as an entrepreneur. And I definitely did not have experience with marketing.

Like Billy, I was someone who followed my passion and was forced to learn marketing—or go back to a desk job.

My Marketing Overwhelm

Of all the sources of information I've consumed, nothing compared to the onslaught I encountered when I first tried to figure out marketing.

The online marketing industry has been around for a long time, with big names promising to teach everything from web design to instructional design to social media marketing to video production to coaching.

It was way too much to learn all at once.

I was listening with dread to all the things the experts were telling me I had to do:

"You need to be on at least seven different social media platforms."

"You need to segment your email marketing."

"You need countdown timers on your sales pages and discounts, but then there's the secret extra discount and the early bird pricing . . ."

In an attempt to make money and get my business off the ground, I was doing everything on the checklist while completely ignoring the fundamental drivers.

I remember signing up for a program in 2015 taught by a very prominent online personality that cost a few thousand dollars, basically titled, "Everything You Will Ever Need to Know to Start and Grow a Successful Business from Scratch." The program was divided into five modules. Not too bad, right?

But each of those modules was like a university degree's worth of knowledge. It took me a full year to understand and implement module one, and another year for module two. A few years later I returned to the course to try to implement the rest of it, but by then it was out of date!

I've spoken to other people who took the same program and never even got past module one. They burned out on the runway, overwhelmed by the dizzying number of details to master before making their first test flight.

So much of the marketing advice found online is about worshiping complexity for the sake of complexity. I see so many complicated funnel diagrams sold by the bundle, as if you can just flip a switch and watch the customers come flooding in.

Self-proclaimed experts hawk their fifteen-stage Facebook ad campaign funnels, targeting ever smaller micro-segments.

As if it were that easy!

I've had an online business for a decade now and have seen so many marketing gurus come and go, all promising to teach you everything under the sun: fancy sales funnels, flashy web design, "secret" landing page templates, sophisticated email sequences, SEO optimization, social media ad-buying ... you could spend a lifetime studying this stuff.

For the average business owner who isn't a marketing whiz, it's all far too complicated and requires far too much maintenance.

Billy and I see online business owners everywhere suffocated by the weight of the fancy systems they've built, and honestly, it's painful to witness. Students, customers, and clients plagued by indecision.

The problems of overwhelm, stress, and anxiety are everywhere. But few careers require you to juggle as many balls simultaneously as running an online business.

And yet, you have goals you want to accomplish. Projects you want to build. Achievements you desire. Impacts you want to make.

At a fundamental level, there is just one thing you need to know to build a financially sustainable business: you must know how to communicate to your prospects in a way that leads them to buy from you.

All the rest are additional layers on this foundation.

My Three ("Smart Person") Mistakes

Smart people tend to have similar hang-ups. And because we can learn more from our mistakes than our wins, let me take you on a trip down memory lane, sharing some of my biggest mistakes in the hope that this advice can help you avoid making the same mistakes on your marketing journey.

(Unfortunately, these memories I retained all too vividly.)

Mistake One: Thinking the Product Will Sell Itself
It's harder to sell a product than make one.

With *Building a Second Brain*, I spent years working harder and harder, believing if I just made the course good enough, somehow the sales would take care of themselves.

Anyone can "make" a course. Slap together some slides and videos, put up a web page, and voilà—you're a course creator!

There are absolutely no requirements to meet or gatekeepers to please, which is the beauty of internet businesses—but also their curse.

Selling your offering is where your well-laid plans collide head-on with reality. People will not part with their money unless you speak in their language, on their terms, to their needs. It's the true test of whether what you've created is sustainable and repeatable—or just a nice art project.

It might not be a course you're selling. It might be a service you produce or coaching, consulting, or software. If you're like the other smart people reading this book, you're an expert in your topic—but not marketing.

You can have every other aspect of your product perfectly designed, but if you don't take the time to understand your customers and how you can help them, no one will ever see it.

If you're an online course creator, you can have the most engaging material, but if people don't finish your course and tell their friends, your business will soon shrivel up.

If you're a coach, you can get life-changing results for clients, but without marketing, the number of people you can help is limited.

If you're a service provider, you could be the best at what you do, but without marketing, only a fraction of the potential market will benefit from your skill.

If you're an author or speaker, you're well aware of how crowded your space is and the importance of standing out.

I know this offends our sensibilities as experts, artists, and creators. We want so badly to believe if we just create something good enough, people will seek it out. It feels wrong that we should have to promote ourselves constantly.

But I'm here to tell you there's no way around it. To maximize your potential, you must do marketing.

Mistake Two: Incorrect Assumptions about Success

Early in my online business journey, I decided to create an online course. I searched online and found popular courses I wanted to emulate.

I noticed they all had these incredible trailer videos. So, I thought, "For my course to be successful, I need a trailer video, too."

I hired a company and spent $5,000 making a fancy promotional video of my own. At the time, the cost was astronomical for me. I had to eat ramen for a month to afford it.

But I thought, "I need to do this right. It has to be perfect. I need to have this big fancy launch, and a fancy launch needs a fancy video."

But none of it resonated with people. They didn't care about the course and didn't buy it, so I wasted that $5,000.

In hindsight, I had preconceived notions about what brings success. I should have validated my idea. I should have tried teaching the course content to at least one person before investing all that money into a fancy video.

I've since learned that production values don't matter until later. Way later.

If you invest a lot of money in your business, whether it be for a fancy video, a new website, or sophisticated graphic design, that does not automatically mean it will pay off.

I thought a spectacular investment would get me spectacular results. No, no, no. You can absolutely spend a lot of money and get terrible results. I learned the hard way that there is little correlation between the two.

Mistake Three: Seeing Marketing as Inherently Bad

The final mistake is a common one. It's the "ick" factor of marketing. Smart people tend to have some of the strongest negative associations with marketing.

I believe one reason for this is because smart people are dedicated to finding the truth, and the field of marketing isn't exactly known for its honesty. That's a turnoff to smart people.

For my audience and entrepreneur friends, integrity is at the heart of everything we do. We don't see our businesses as a way to make a quick buck. We want to see change made in the world, and we believe we can make it.

Yet, creating change requires selling our ideas. And so many smart people are turned off by selling. Many readers of this book, perhaps yourself included, have had a bad experience with a salesperson that tainted their association with sales forever.

Here's the mindset shift I want to offer: nothing about sales or marketing is inherently bad. It's how they're often done that's bad. And most people throw out the baby with the bathwater because when they think of marketing, they immediately bring to mind the sleazy used car salesman or the scammy internet marketer.

On the flip side, the best marketing we encounter we *don't even think of as marketing*. Your home is filled with products you love, and it's unlikely you remember the marketing material that led you to buy those products.

This makes your job here more difficult because you have to ignore all the examples of marketing that readily come to mind—the icky examples—and emulate ones you may not even notice.

Luckily, there's a solution around that. Rather than copy and paste marketing examples you find in the wild into your business, learn the timeless principles of marketing instead. That way, when you do come across marketing in the real world, you'll be able to discern if and how to best borrow that idea.

Going forward, I encourage you to reframe your view of marketing. Instead of thinking marketing is deception, I want you to think of marketing as teaching. You are teaching people how to value your product.

Once you drop any cynicism you have around what you're doing and see marketing for what it's supposed to be, you'll feel a new sense of freedom. You'll see you can market yourself and your offerings in a way that's aligned with your values by being honest with and teaching your audience about what you do, and skip the ick.

This is not an easy task, especially after years of seeing so many awful examples of marketing. But trust me, it gets easier. I promise you'll find your way. The approach we give you in this book will set you on the right path.

Chapter Three

The Upstream/ Downstream Marketing Metaphor

By **Billy Broas**

I was speaking at a conference and asked my audience a simple question: What is marketing?

One by one, people shouted back:

- Facebook ads!
- Social media!
- Webinars!
- Coupons!
- Going viral!

I've asked this question before and the responses are always the same—they're all over the place. Ask ten people to define marketing and you'll get eleven answers.

Search online and you'll confirm this. You'll find endless software, courses, training, tools, experts, and companies offering to help you improve the items in the list above and so much more.

For our smart person business owner with a packed calendar and, say, a ninety-minute block of time each week to devote to marketing, what should you focus on first?

In those ninety minutes, should you work on Facebook ads? Social media accounts? Webinars? Are each of these created equal?

With infinite ways to improve our marketing, we must expect some marketing tasks to matter more than others. It's unlikely the same ninety minutes invested into one type of task will yield the same results as ninety minutes put into another.

This is why, when you have limited time to devote to marketing, prioritization is critical.

Some marketing tasks *must* be given priority, but which ones?

Each business owner's needs will vary, but for now, let's set aside our individual areas for improvement and explore some bigger questions:

Are there certain areas of marketing that can give you a bigger bang for your buck?

Are there enduring rules that can guide us to focus on what truly matters? Yes.

To give you a better understanding of the marketing landscape, I'd like to introduce you to my Upstream vs. Downstream metaphor. Do you remember the endless answers to my question, "What is marketing?"

This metaphor will help you categorize those responses.

When you categorize marketing activities, you'll be able to see where each marketing activity fits in the big picture, and as a result, you'll understand the impact of each one.

You'll make smarter decisions about how to focus your marketing time and how to prioritize your marketing tasks to create a comprehensive marketing plan. When you sit down for that weekly marketing session, you'll have more confidence that what you're doing matters, and you're going to see the results of that focus.

The Upstream vs. Downstream Marketing Metaphor

Visualize marketing as a mighty river. Picture our river with three major sections: upstream, midstream, and downstream. Each river section plays a vital role in our marketing efforts.

Let's begin the journey.

Upstream: Your Core Message

When you're standing in the middle, every river has an upstream and a downstream. Upstream is where we find the source of the river, its origin. Like the river, your marketing requires a source, a core message from which all marketing activities flow.

What is a core message? It's the central argument for why someone should choose your product or service.

Think of your core message as the underground spring of your marketing river. It's not visible to your customers, but it's essential for providing direction and coherence to all your marketing efforts. This message should be well documented and referred to whenever you create new marketing material.

For something as important as your core marketing message, you need a high degree of quality. This isn't one of those areas where good enough is good enough. Skip this step and the marketing material you send downstream will have reduced effectiveness.

A core messaging document is not a brand manual. A brand manual dictates a business' visuals, like its logo, fonts, and colors. A core messaging document, on the other hand, focuses on the beliefs your prospects need to hold for your product to be an obvious purchase.

We'll help you identify those beliefs starting in Chapter Six. It's the one activity that will give you the biggest bang for your buck with marketing.

For now, let's continue down the river and focus on the next two sections. Here is where many smart people get stuck.

Midstream: Marketing Channels

As the river flows downhill from its source, it branches out. Some branches go right and some go left. For our metaphor, these branches represent marketing channels. You might think of them as distribution channels or social media platforms that transport your core message to your prospects.

Many people mistakenly equate the totality of marketing with marketing channels.

Let me challenge you further and say these are not merely marketing channels, platforms, or whatever term the kids are using these days; these channels include whole ecosystems. And these ecosystems are teeming with life. Here, messages are exchanged, relationships are built, and goods and services are sold.

Below, you'll find a list of twenty marketing channels.

20 Marketing Channels

1. YouTube
2. Podcasts
3. Email newsletters
4. Facebook
5. Instagram
6. X (formerly Twitter)
7. Pinterest
8. LinkedIn
9. TikTok
10. SEO
11. Pay-per-click advertising
12. Text messaging
13. Amazon
14. TV commercials
15. Direct mail
16. Billboards
17. Newspapers
18. Bus benches
19. Trade shows
20. Conferences

If you think about the human experience, it's no surprise that we often equate marketing with channels.

Thirty years ago, we had marketing channels, but they weren't so pervasive. You'd see a newspaper on your driveway when you walked to your mailbox. You'd see a TV commercial when you sat down to relax after dinner.

Today, we encounter marketing channels relentlessly. Unlock your smartphone and hundreds of them will stare back at you. Facebook, X, Instagram, Google Search.

Have you noticed that our most frequently used smartphone apps are also the largest marketing channels? As a result, those apps are what we often associate with marketing. However, the smart marketer knows to put those apps in perspective—they aren't everything.

The smart marketer knows marketing is far more than channels or advertisements. The smart marketer knows that 90% of their hard work is done before their ad appears on their customer's social media feed.

Sure, many internet gurus love to preach that there is one channel you *must* be on. "Are you *really* not using LinkedIn? You're missing out!" they say.

(Their survival depends on instilling FOMO.)

Many of them claim to be marketing experts, but they are not. They are *channel* experts. There's a difference. And now that you know the river metaphor, you know the distinction.

Smart marketers take the following mindset toward marketing channels:

- They put most of their effort into creating a compelling core message.
- They don't put too much hope into a single marketing channel. They test multiple channels.
- When they find a channel that works, they double down on that channel until it fails to deliver an acceptable return on investment.

Compare this mindset to the following advice:

"TikTok is where it's at!"

"You've GOT to join Threads."

"If you want to make real money, you need to be on Instagram."

I'm not saying to ignore these claims the next time you hear them, but know that channels come and go. Never make the mistake of thinking your success rides on a single marketing channel.

How to Spot Advice around Channels

To help reduce your marketing overwhelm and keep your eye on the biggest needle movers, learn how to spot when you're being given advice specific to channels, not broadly on marketing.

Below, you'll find a few headlines of articles that should make your inner voice say, "I'm getting advice about marketing channels."

- "5 Tips to Go Viral on Instagram"
- "This Year's Most Important Updates to Facebook Ads"
- "How to Optimize Your YouTube Thumbnails for Maximum Clicks"
- "13 SEO Tips for Higher Rankings"
- "Podcast Promotion Strategies"

Do you see how each article is referring to a marketing channel?

There are millions of articles like this. For me, when growing my first online business, reading these types of articles became overwhelming.

I was even printing off these articles and stacking them on my desk in a desperate attempt to learn it all.

Well, here's the good news: you can ignore 99% of these articles until your core message is set.

Focus on your core message first. Only then will those articles make a difference.

With channels now addressed, let's look at our downstream section. This next section is where we find what's commonly known as "shiny objects."

Downstream: Marketing Tactics

Back to our river metaphor, let's continue our journey downstream.

In this part of the journey, you begin to employ tactics. Think of tactics as specific actions you take to steer, avoid obstacles, and take advantage of the river's flow. A tactic could be choosing the right paddle stroke or deciding how to navigate around a fallen tree.

In marketing, tactics are the specific actions and techniques you use to reach your audience and achieve your goals. Just like in paddling, selecting the right marketing tactic is crucial. However, these tactics only make a difference if you're clear on your destination.

Tactics are only effective if your core message is dialed in. Without a clear direction and understanding of your target audience's needs and how you intend to meet them, the most skillful tactics are like paddling aggressively without knowing which way the river flows. You might spend a lot of energy, but you won't necessarily get to your desired destination efficiently—or at all.

Below, you'll find a list of common marketing tactics that you might recognize.

20 Marketing Tactics

1. Viral giveaways	11. Two-step opt-ins
2. Online contests	12. Retargeting ads
3. Website quizzes	13. Referral programs
4. Website pop-ups	14. Guest blogging
5. Push notifications	15. Themed social media days
6. Guest blogging	16. Online communities
7. Upsells	17. Mobile optimization
8. Downsells	18. Voice search
9. Chatbots	19. Hashtags
10. Video marketing	20. Cart abandonment emails

Look familiar?

Similar to our list of marketing channels, marketing tactics are endless. Once again, you can press the pause button on obsessing over the list.

It's not that you don't *need* tactics. But after creating many marketing campaigns, I can tell you the items on that list aren't the big needle movers. They're a better fit for finding incremental gains after you've already got traction.

Once, I took on a client who had recently paid a freelancer $10,000 to build a Facebook advertising sales funnel. The Facebook setup was impressive. It had all sorts of if-then statements, retargeting, and upsells and downsells.

But the funnel didn't generate a single sale. Not one. And the reason was obvious: all the attention went into the fancy Facebook setup and none went into the messaging inside that funnel.

It was only after his $10,000 was spent that the business owner hired me to help him. We wrote a simple (but well-thought-out) email campaign that brought in $40,000 over a couple of weeks.

This story highlights the difference between a fancy marketing setup with weak messaging versus a simple marketing setup (nothing but emails) with strong messaging. I'll take strong messaging over a fancy setup any day.

After that successful email campaign, my client then deployed his new messaging across his website, social media accounts, and yes, his Facebook ads. After implementing the new messaging across all platforms, he saw a significant boost in engagement and conversions.

When you begin by dialing in your core message, all of those shiny objects work better.

How to Spot Advice around Tactics

If you see articles like the ones below, you know you're about to encounter advice around tactics:

- "Unlock the Power of Viral Giveaways"
- "Five Creative Ways to Use Website Pop-ups"
- "Proven Templates for Cart Abandonment Emails"
- "Chatbots: Uplevel Your Customer Service Game"
- "Stay Top of Mind with Push Notifications"

Tempting, aren't they? Heck, I'd like to read a couple of those.

But again—we must resist the dopamine hits. These tactics are like candy for the mind, and we know that a diet consisting only of candy, while rewarding in the short-term, is not the best long-term.

If you're like the typical reader of this book, you're not looking for a quick fix; you're looking for long-term, sustainable business growth. To achieve it, you must prioritize your attention upstream to your core message first.

Go Upstream

We've established that you and I have a tendency to dive into details and get stuck. So, when it comes to marketing, we must do everything we can to resist running off to obsess over our website, install all the plugins, and mindlessly start cranking out content.

Instead, pause and take the time to do the upfront work. Yes, you have permission to stop *doing* and spend time *thinking*.

How should you spend this upfront time? Your solution will be similar to mine in my brewing story . . .

Just as my solution was to give myself the space to focus on the raw ingredients in my beer, your time is best spent on your raw ingredients. In marketing, your raw ingredients are the components of your core message.

With your core message in place, you can then make the best use of whichever channels and tactics you employ.

You can now hopefully see how marketing—once chaotic, random, and overwhelming—actually has order. The river metaphor puts everything into perspective.

And now, for your core messaging . . . what should it do? What should it accomplish?

The next chapter will show you.

CHAPTER FOUR

The One Question That Makes Marketing Simple

By BILLY BROAS

In the 1990s, a guy from Ohio named Joe started a carpet cleaning business in his hometown. He was a couple of years into the business, and he was dead broke—sales weren't coming in.

He tried offering discounts and coupons, but the uptake rate wasn't as high as expected. Discount strategies just weren't working, and any takers he had wiped out his profit.

Brainstorming about the problem, Joe realized that most people in his town simply didn't "get" the value of cleaning their carpets.

For example, his potential customers didn't realize that carpets:

- Are 4,000 times dirtier than a toilet seat.
- Could harbor mold, which can be harmful to your health.
- Are one of the leading causes of asthma.

Joe decided to try a different strategy. Instead of selling, he would educate.

His potential clients couldn't understand the importance of cleaning their carpets unless they understood what was at stake. No one wants to get sick or walk around on something dirty. Joe's prospects didn't know these facts, so he decided to teach them.

He wrote articles explaining why it's important to get your carpets cleaned, how often to clean them, and how to know your carpets are being cleaned correctly.

This educational material became his marketing material.

Once Joe finished creating his educational marketing material, he began sharing it with his town's residents. Almost immediately, Joe's phone began to ring. Orders poured in, with people pleading for Joe to come clean their carpets as soon as possible.

What happened?

Before, Joe had relied on marketing tactics, but didn't have a core message.

Joe needed a core message to share with his potential clients, something they could see themselves in. Otherwise, he'd simply be another salesman trying to con them out of their hard-earned money. But if they could see how Joe fit into their lives, they'd appreciate the value of his offering.

Once Joe understood the core message his clients needed to hear, he was able to communicate with them in a way they could grab on to.

While his competitors' marketing was nothing but sales pitches, Joe's marketing became education. As a result, Joe attracted clients away from his competitors. And the people who didn't buy from Joe were at least better informed.

Joe finally turned a profit and his business only grew from there. He turned his one-man carpet cleaning company into a million-dollar business, employing dozens of people and becoming well known within his industry. He was even asked to speak at industry conferences and was showered with awards.

How did Joe go from losing money to becoming a massive success? He asked the all-important question:

What does my prospect need to believe in order to buy?

That question—What does my prospect need to believe in order to buy?—is the only question you need to ask yourself to develop your core message.

You'll take your answers to this question and use them to create your marketing material. We call this entire process **Belief Building**.

One easy way to think about Belief Building is as a sophisticated form of objection handling. If you removed all the prospect's objections to buying, they would have no logical choice but to buy from you.

Typically, business training teaches you to handle your prospect's objections at the point of sale. Belief Building takes the concept of your potential customer's objections and deals with them earlier in the customer's journey.

But more than that, Belief Building goes beyond simply addressing objections; it actively educates prospects on the value and relevance of your offerings.

Rather than passively waiting for prospects to buy, Belief Building actively guides them through a learning process and gives them the education they need to ultimately invest into your product or service.

By the end of this journey, they are not just buying; they are making an informed and confident decision to become a customer, fully convinced of your value proposition.

Belief Building first gets you *buy-in*. Buy-in naturally leads to *buyers*.

This is what legendary management consultant Peter Drucker meant when he wrote in his 1993 book, *Management*, "The aim of marketing is to make selling superfluous."[1]

Do you see how this is welcome news for the smart person?

Belief Building gives you an alternative to hard selling. Who wants to twist arms and be pushy? When you do marketing correctly, the sale becomes a natural conclusion of the customer journey. Belief Building melts away your prospect's resistance to buying your product.

With Belief Building, your role shifts from a seller to an educator and a guide.

Our approach is tailor-made for the smart person who isn't looking for a get-rich-quick scheme, but is in it for the long run. When you're not convincing someone to buy, but rather leading them to recognize what you offer is exactly what they've been looking for, you gain customers who are more likely to remain loyal, engaged, and satisfied with their decision. And they'll buy from you again and again.

This approach not only elevates the quality of your customer base, but also enhances the sustainability of your business. Your customers don't just make a purchase; they form a lasting relationship with you.

---

1   Peter Drucker, *Management* (Routledge, 2012).

They're the kind of customers who become loyal advocates, spreading the word about your products and services because they believe in them, not just because they got a good deal.

Belief Building is the upstream task that makes everything downstream work better.

History's Great Copywriters Knew This

I'm a student of history and am obsessed with uncovering lost wisdom. When we modern people start patting ourselves on the back for our cutting-edge advancements, I worry.

"What might we be forgetting?" I ask.

In the realm of marketing, we've forgotten a crucial element: the art of copywriting.

Copywriting is about crafting a compelling argument for why someone should choose your product. It's a key skill for boosting sales through your website, emails, and other marketing materials. However, many mistakenly believe that copywriting is all about clickbait headlines and over-the-top promises.

The truth is, the best copywriters rely on more than flashy tactics. They understand the power of education and the importance of connecting with your reader on a deeper level.

So, why do I study the great copywriters of the past? It's not necessarily because they were more naturally talented. It's because they operated under favorable constraints. And these constraints helped them create lessons that apply through the ages.

Consider a copywriter from the 1950s. Without the luxury of email or the internet, they had to craft sales letters, print them, stuff them into envelopes, purchase stamps, and send them through the mail. This process demanded careful consideration of every word, as each one came with a cost.

Who is more likely to master the craft of copywriting? The 1950s copywriter who had to invest time and money into each letter, or the modern copywriter who can send out 100,000 emails at virtually no cost?

The answer is the 1950s copywriter. Their constraints forced them to focus on the quality of their writing, rather than getting distracted by the plethora of tools and platforms available today.

When each word costs money, you put more thought and effort into what you write.

The lesson is clear: **when looking to solve a problem, consider those who faced constraints that led to the best solutions.**

As I grappled with the complexities of marketing and tried various strategies, I found this Belief Building approach aligns beautifully with the methodologies of history's great copywriters.

One copywriter, in particular, emphasized the crucial role of establishing beliefs in the minds of prospects before pitching a product.

Eugene Schwartz

Eugene Schwartz (1927–1995) is considered one of the greatest copywriters who ever lived. His book, *Breakthrough Advertising* (1966), is considered the Bible of copywriting.

In the book, Schwartz warns against using those big, hype-filled promises you see everywhere today. Readers don't believe those gigantic promises, Schwartz says, so instead of making them, what you should do instead is—build belief.

"Belief is the goal," Schwartz teaches.

A person's beliefs are shaped by their opinions, attitudes, and past experiences. When writing marketing campaigns for his clients, Schwartz often began by addressing the customer's belief systems.

He researched his prospects and discovered any false beliefs that might prevent them from purchasing his product. Schwartz tells the story of his attempt to sell a repair manual for an appliance you likely have in your household today.

Selling a TV Repair Manual in the 1950s

In the 1950s, Schwartz faced the same problem you now face. You know your product works—but how do you convince your prospects of that?

Schwartz took on a client who was an electronics expert. His client had written a TV repair manual for men and women across America, showing them how to fix common TV malfunctions. His client had proven the manual's effectiveness with a test group of customers.

Now, it was time to sell the repair manual to the mass market.

The problem? Most people didn't believe they could make TV repairs themselves.

In the 1950s, TVs were big, heavy, complex machines. They broke down constantly, and their owners had to then call in an expert, which led to expensive repair bills.

If you could repair the TV yourself, you'd save a ton of money.

But how do you sell a TV repair manual to people who don't believe they can make the repairs? You can't. Not unless you clear up their false beliefs.

Schwartz realized that before he could sell the TV repair manual, he first needed to instill the belief that his prospect had the ability to repair the TV. Without this mental acceptance, it didn't matter how much he sweetened his offer. It didn't matter if he offered a 50% discount on the repair manual if his prospects didn't believe they could use the product.

Schwartz wrote a sales letter that used a Belief Building strategy similar to what you're about to learn, and he turned the TV repair manual into a massive success.

Your product isn't a TV repair manual, but do you see how you face the same challenge as Schwartz? You know your product works, but how do you get your prospects to believe that and take a chance with you?

Once you realize that your prospects don't hold the beliefs required to accept your offer, your task switches from selling to Belief Building.

You ask the all-important question, "What does my customer need to believe in order to buy?"

How This Question Simplifies Marketing

Remember, smart people have a tendency to overcomplicate. In your field, you've benefited from diving deep into your topic. You've taken the time to learn the nuances and distinctions, and craft the best solutions.

But when it comes to marketing those solutions, your closeness to your topic becomes a drawback. Your prospect isn't ready for all those details and distinctions. You've diverged your topic into so many subtopics that when you go to present your solution to your prospect, you don't even know where to start.

As a result, you give way too many details, jump around too much when you speak with prospects, or get so overwhelmed you don't even try. Each of these is a common occurrence when smart people are tasked with explaining what they do.

Due to the curse of knowledge, you're more likely to lose prospects—people you could have helped.

If divergence is the problem, convergence is the solution. Convergence is the antidote to complexity and your path back to simplicity. It's not dumbing things down, because the depth and complexity remains, but you simply shouldn't lead with the details. Those come in later.

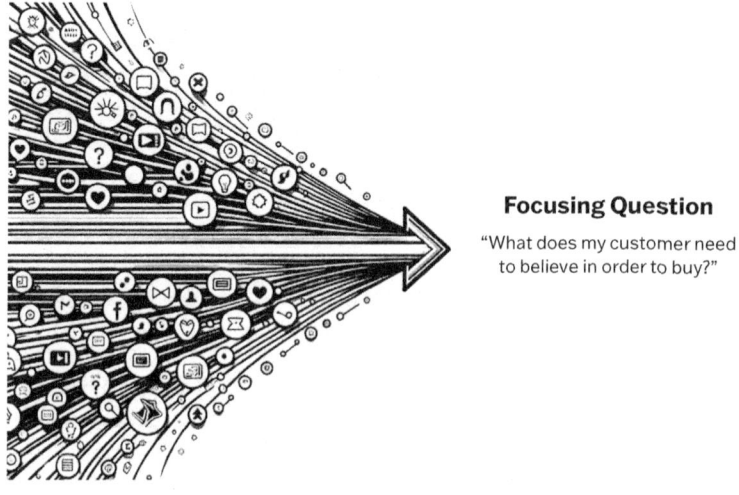

Focusing Question
"What does my customer need to believe in order to buy?"

© Simple Marketing for Smart People

Rather than disperse your energy across the endless landscape of marketing channels and tactics, focus your analytical mind on solving this single problem.

The Power of a Focusing Question

Much has been written about the benefits of a focusing question, and how to zero in on that one important thing. Gary Keller famously wrote about it in his book titled, *The One Thing*.

When faced with a challenge, Keller recommends we ask, "What's the one thing I can do that makes everything else easier?"

This type of question—a focusing question—is the perfect solution for the smart person. It focuses your divergent mind and deep knowledge in your area of expertise on a single goal.

Let's see how this new way of looking at marketing aligns with our upstream vs. downstream metaphor.

Earlier, we showed marketing as a river. Upstream is where your most important work is done, which is to create your core message. You now see that Belief Building is how we go about it.

The better you build these beliefs into your core message, the more effective everything you send downstream becomes. Your Facebook ads convert better, your opt-in pages get more subscribers, and your social share buttons get more clicks.

Let's look at a visual.

Upstream	Midstream	Downstream
Answer this question to guide your **core messaging:**	Distribute your messaging across these **channels:**	Amplify your message using these **tactics:**
What does my customer need to believe in order to buy?	• Facebook • Podcasts • YouTube • SEO • Email • and more	• Website pop-ups • Giveaways • Hashtags • Retargeting ads • Chatbots • and more

When you begin with your focusing question, everything downstream works better.

When sitting down to work on your marketing, use this table to help you prioritize your efforts.

Now that you understand the idea behind Belief Building and how it can increase sales, let's look at an alternative method that's often resorted to.

How Effective is a Coupon without Belief?

Remember in our carpet cleaning story, when Joe began offering coupons in an attempt to land new customers?

Well, if someone doesn't believe cleaning their carpets is important, how effective is a coupon? Would offering a customer a 15% discount make much of a difference if the person doesn't believe in the value of carpet cleaning?

Let's say we're convinced coupons will increase sales, so we decide to discount even more. After all, 15% off isn't too big a discount, so we give our prospects a 50% discount. We'll sell a few more people, but now we have other problems:

1. We've sliced into our profit margins.
2. The customer *still* doesn't believe what we're doing is very important.

With the second point, how good of a customer will this person be in the long run? How likely are they to buy again? How likely are they to refer friends?

Discounting may get us better sales figures, but it doesn't get us better customers. When we discount, we're more likely to attract headaches.

Have you noticed that often the customers who pay the least require the most attention, while the ones who pay the most are a dream to work with?

One of the most welcome benefits of Belief Building is that you will attract more of those dream customers.

So please, stop printing coupons, giving deals, and making concessions. When you focus on Belief Building, you won't need to.

Recap of Belief Building

The best prospects to pitch to are the ones who have the beliefs needed to buy. You can—and should—be the one to instill those beliefs.

You do so through your marketing content. You first ask the question, "What does my customer need to believe in order to buy?" Your answer to that question goes into a core messaging document. You then turn that document into informative and educational marketing material.

Your marketing material then makes a clear, compelling, and honest argument for your solution. Your newly informed prospect will understand and appreciate your argument. They will buy into the case you make for your product or service and many of them will ultimately purchase your product or service.

Let's recap our key definitions so it's all clear:

Upstream vs. Downstream: our metaphor for understanding the marketing landscape. It helps us:

1. Categorize any marketing tips, advice, or tools we come across.
2. Prioritize our marketing efforts.

Belief Building: The process of bringing a prospect to the point where they fully understand and value our offer. Buying from us becomes their only logical choice.

Belief Building is done through your core message, which can be sent down any marketing channel and can include any marketing tactic.

Next, we'll cover the steps in Belief Building, which are:

1. Identify your prospects' current beliefs.
2. Identify the beliefs required for the purchase to be obvious.
3. Create the marketing content that builds those required beliefs.

The following visual helps explain our process.

The River Metaphor for Marketing

Upstream   **Downstream**

The Focusing Question   **Channels**
"What does my customer need to   The places where you distribute
believe in order to buy?"   your Belief Building marketing
                                      content: Your website, Facebook,
                                      emails, ads, etc.

Belief Building   **Tactics**
The act of educating your   Actions that amplify your market-
prospect so the purchase of your   ing: Share buttons, countdown
product or service is obvious   timers, etc.

Now let's see how Belief Building is applied to a real-life business. In the next chapter, Tiago will share how he uses Belief Building to guide the content he creates for his products.

CHAPTER FIVE

How I Use Belief Building

By TIAGO FORTE

I'd been in business for six years and was finally able to pay the bills. But when I looked at what it would take to get to the next level, I had no idea where to even begin.

My students constantly told me how much my course had transformed their relationship to knowledge and information. Many said it was the best educational experience of their lives.

And yet, every time I heard another glowing testimonial, I would think, "If it's so good, why aren't more people buying?"

Despite the wonderful highs of compliments, of success, of results created for my customers, I had also gotten really used to the lows. Every Monday morning I woke up with a fresh batch of support emails to answer. I was the only person on staff, so responding to each and every one fell on me.

If I was having trouble finding the time to answer customer support requests, how would I ever carve out the bandwidth to tackle a whole new arena like marketing?

I was responsible for everything in my business—designing the slides, keeping track of time, managing the Q&A, and you know, teaching the course. While it was exhilarating to pursue my passion, the burden of having to do it all myself felt like a crushing weight on my shoulders.

All of this meant my business was not growing. Its growth was constrained by revenue because until I made more money, I couldn't hire people to delegate my responsibilities to, or invest in better software platforms, or upgrade our customer experience, or heck, buy my wife and me a vacation.

I knew I had something powerful in my course, but without the ability to sell and market myself effectively, expand my audience, and grow my price points, everything felt stuck.

I had already done the hard part—creating something good—but didn't know how to capitalize on the opportunity it created for me. It was this continual feeling of loss and frustration, missed chances, and FOMO— like having my hands tied behind my back as a feast was laid out before me—that finally pushed me over the edge to learn what felt like the least interesting field in the world: marketing.

At the time, I thought marketing consisted of adding more countdown timers, exclamation points, and big red banners to my website. I begrudgingly tried a variety of tactics, but without a central message or strategy, even the accidental successes I hit on taught me nothing.

One day, in the midst of this confusion and frustration, the company that hosted my courses, Teachable, put on an event featuring online education experts, and both Billy and I were invited.

Billy, being a fellow productivity nerd, had taken my course a couple of years before, although I didn't recognize his name. After the Teachable event, he reached out.

"Hey Tiago, I took your online course and loved it. More people should know about what you're doing, and I've got some ideas. Want to chat?"

Frankly, I needed the help. I was stuck at a plateau. You might be in a similar position where you're finding it hard to expand beyond your inner circle of superfans. Many smart people find themselves in this position. Superfans' enthusiasm is almost a false positive. It takes a completely different approach to go beyond that hardcore group and sell to people who've never heard of you.

Billy and I chatted and I learned that he was like me, a non-marketer who was forced to learn marketing. He was trying to succeed with his beer brewing website, just like I was with my productivity website. I learned the challenges Billy faced, how he had found what worked, and how he'd helped many people I knew.

He explained that true marketing isn't all those gimmicks and random tactics. Marketing is teaching, and as a fellow nerd, Billy told me I was well suited to thrive in marketing. I agreed with him on the nerdy part, but I wasn't sure about the marketing part. That seemed like a stretch. Still, I decided to give it a shot.

Billy and I came to an arrangement, and in the summer of 2019, I hired him to help me improve my marketing efforts. It was a significant investment—the most I had spent on my business since that ill-fated trailer video—and part of me wondered whether I was making a similar mistake.

Thankfully, I made a wise decision.

One of the first things Billy taught me was Belief Building. He didn't have his upstream versus downstream metaphor back then (I love it, by the way), but he emphasized that most of my care and attention should go into building belief through my marketing content. All the other stuff I was obsessed with, like which social media platform to post on and which website plugins I should install, took a back seat.

When it comes to Belief Building, the fact that something from a century ago could work just as well today is all the proof I needed. This attitude was completely in line with my trust in timeless, evergreen principles that don't change with the next software update.

The concept of Belief Building immediately made sense to me because it is exactly what happens in teaching. If a student has the right beliefs, they will have no problem mastering the subject being taught. Likewise, if your customer has the right beliefs, taking you up on your offer will be a no-brainer. If they don't have those beliefs, then no amount of discounting or promoting or creating urgency will get them across the finish line.

Here are some of the beliefs I came up with when I first did the Belief Building exercise for my online course, *Building a Second Brain*:

- My brain is for having ideas, not holding them.
- I am already creative and do creative work.
- My thoughts and ideas are valuable and worth saving and revisiting.
- I am already doing most of the work required.
- I can get and stay organized quickly and easily.
- If I don't make an intentional effort to preserve my thinking, it will be lost.

If any of these beliefs are missing in the minds of my potential customers, there's no way they will even consider a course like mine.

They could believe my course is the best thing in the world for others, but if they don't believe "My brain is for having ideas, not holding them," then what I'm offering won't make sense for them.

They can think having a Second Brain is the niftiest idea they've ever heard, but it will remain only a nice-to-have until they agree that "If I don't make an intentional effort to preserve my thinking, it will be lost."

Belief Building also revealed exactly which content I should create. I realized I could now create specific pieces of content to cultivate each belief.

I could systematically create alignment with a large group of people using informative and empowering content, instead of drowning them in endless how-to tutorials.

That is how you know every hour you spend creating content is worth it. Without this approach as your guide, how else can you be certain that every piece of content your reader consumes will move them decisively toward a purchase?

Put yourself in the mind of your customer. What do they need to not only know but *believe in* and *agree with* to trust you with their money?

This Belief Building approach also has the wonderful side effect of making hard selling unnecessary because your prospects are already pre-sold by the time they reach the checkout page.

What to Expect with Belief Building

A heads up: as you do your Belief Building exercises, you are going to create content that may feel very basic. You may even feel like you're "dumbing down" your ideas.

That's a good thing.

Rather than think of it as dumbing down, think of it as distilling, refining, boiling it down, finding the essence, or finding the signal in the noise. Those are all more helpful ways of describing what you'll actually be doing with your marketing content.

Still, smart people resist this advice tremendously.

Because if you make it too simple, your content will lose value, right? Or, if it's really that simple, anyone could understand it, and then what's your added value? What is your contribution?

Consider this: diving straight into the full complexity of your topic displays a lack of empathy for your customer. Is it more important for you to have your expertise and authority validated, or for them to get the benefits you promised? Don't attach your identity to the details and complexity of your topic. Your value goes far beyond that.

Too often, we simply fail to see things from our customer's point of view. We fail to understand they are at a different stage than we are. They probably need something simple and easy to understand. The nuances can come later.

To make it as business owners, we must ask:

- What stage is my reader at?
- What's their readiness for the next step?
- What is that next step or milestone?
- How can I meet them where they are?

You must trust that once your potential customer gets to the next step, they will have the wisdom and the self-determination to figure out what's next for them—even if it doesn't involve you.

Bridge the Gap

The thing that's so powerful about Belief Building is that often, as smart people, we are of two minds.

On one hand, we're doing a lot of what we call marketing. We're creating content, going on webinars, publishing YouTube videos, and writing copy.

And then, on the other hand, we are teaching and delivering the content. But how does someone go from a stranger being marketed to one minute, and then the next minute they are a student inside the classroom? The process that goes on in people's minds to have them say, "Yes, I'm in," is often largely a mystery to us as business owners.

The Belief Building question, "What does my customer need to believe to buy?" gave me the realization that this journey can be understood. It can be studied and mapped. And once you do that, you can improve it, amplify it, strengthen it, and patch over its holes.

The customer journey begins long before someone buys your product, and extends well through the delivery of your product. Many beliefs are needed along that journey.

For example, with my online course, I need my potential students to say to themselves, "Even if I miss a live call, I can still get value from the program." If I fail to instill that belief, then some people won't purchase solely because they have a scheduling conflict with one of the live sessions, which, in my opinion, is a tragedy—they were almost to the starting line and then tripped over a tiny pebble.

Belief Building gave me a few more realizations:

- People can be trusted to make good decisions for themselves if they're presented with the truth.
- Creating mountains of free content doesn't necessarily help the prospect and may actually hurt you.
- Missing one belief can derail the whole sale. (This is a wild thing to witness. For my course, if they have 99.9% of the beliefs, but think online courses don't work, then there's no way they will buy.)

In addition to missing beliefs, you can also be sabotaged by a false belief. Oh boy, do I have a story about that.

Blindsided by a False Belief

In one round of my course, I was blindsided by a belief that came out of nowhere.

There was a whole group of academics who had joined the course. They came out in one live session and in unison said, "Your course is promoting plagiarism."

Out of nowhere!

They said, "You're telling us to copy and paste things and clip them into our Second Brain? You are promoting plagiarism!"

I thought, "I have never heard that before."

It blindsided me, and our entire team, and we had to address it in that live session. Then we had to address it more in the next live session.

This group almost caused a revolt, which, as you can imagine, almost derailed the whole program. After the storm had passed, however, I came to realize this seeming disagreement was actually a demonstration of how much those academics cared.

Think of the beliefs driving their behavior:

- Academic integrity matters.
- Citing your sources is important.
- Honesty is an essential part of creating knowledge.

These are totally valid beliefs that we agreed on. And as a result of that mini-revolt, I added more content into my marketing and my course supporting these beliefs.

You see, for this group of academics, there was a gap between their existing beliefs and the beliefs required to be successful with my course. And it was my responsibility to bridge that gap.

I showed them that not only is using a Second Brain system not plagiarism, but a Second Brain *fights against* plagiarism. A Second Brain helps you better keep track of your sources, so you can cite them accurately without losing track of where they came from.

Once they saw me demonstrate this, the revolt was quelled, and this group of academics became loyal advocates.

I turned that objection into a strength. Many business owners would ignore this objection, hoping it would go away. I faced it head-on, flipped it around, and now my credibility among academics is higher because I've addressed their need to maintain the integrity of their knowledge.

How This Simplifies Marketing

The problem with marketing is it's highly divergent. As Billy mentioned, when you dive into marketing, everything begins to multiply.

In comparison, the Belief Building question is convergent. It brings order by reducing the number of things you're doing rather than expanding them.

Now you have a bridge that all your prospects must cross. It doesn't matter whether they're beginner-level or advanced.

When creating any new piece of content, I now ask, "Which belief is this going to instill or strengthen?" If I can't find one, or if I already have a lot of content that reinforces that belief, I forget it. It wouldn't be a good return on investment for my time.

Every time I create a piece of content or go on someone's podcast, I want to be plugging the holes in people's belief systems. It's like getting a little cork and putting it in one of those leaks.

My core messaging document is a Google Doc that now has over 100 beliefs. That may seem like a lot, but plenty of business owners have documents with over 100 content ideas. I used to be the same way, writing down every random content idea I could think of, which is like throwing spaghetti at the wall.

Now, armed with my 100+ beliefs, my content has *direction*. Rather than being random, I know my mission: to instill the beliefs needed for my prospects to buy.

You'll begin with that first step: identify where your audience is now.

CHAPTER SIX

Identifying Your Customer's Existing Beliefs

By BILLY BROAS

Now you know your mission: build the beliefs required for the purchase of your product to be obvious. When you do so, you remove every mental roadblock that prevents your prospect from buying.

In addition to gaining new customers, this approach leads to a number of additional benefits:

1. Because you'll have more buy-in from your prospects, you won't need to hard-sell.
2. Because your prospects are pre-sold on what you offer, they'll be more likely to act upon your advice, use your product, have success, and tell their friends.
3. With this approach, marketing becomes more like education. That's music to the ears of the smart person.

Simply put, this approach is a better way of doing marketing. That's because it's what marketing is supposed to be, as opposed to the flash, hype, tactics, and gimmicks it's so often confused with.

Now, how do we put this new marketing approach into practice? First, we must uncover your customer's current beliefs. That's your starting point.

I've heard people say, "You can't change someone's beliefs." Really? You can *never* change someone's beliefs? Of course you can.

When people say, "You can't change someone's beliefs," they mean it can be *difficult* to change someone's beliefs, which is true. The question then becomes: how difficult?

Well, the degree of difficulty depends on how deep-seated the belief is. Is the belief lightly held or something deeply ingrained?

Remember, in the end, we're only doing marketing. We're not trying to change someone's religious beliefs or core values. Think back to our carpet cleaning example and ask yourself, what's a tougher task, convincing someone to change religions, or to clean their carpets?

See what I mean?

Heck, I bet after you learned carpets are generally dirtier than a toilet seat, you were at least 1% more likely to clean your carpets. It wasn't too difficult to change your mind on that belief, was it?

That said, even in marketing, some Belief Building jobs are tougher than others. As much as possible, you want to speak to people who already have most of the beliefs required to buy from you. In other words, you'll want to preach to the choir.

When you speak to people who are largely in agreement with you, you can expedite the customer journey. This doesn't necessarily mean your services become faster, but rather that your prospects progress more quickly toward a decision. This efficiency benefits both you and your prospects.

For you, the business owner, this means less time spent trying to convince those who may never align with your perspective. Your efforts can be focused on potential customers who are already predisposed to accept what you offer, allowing you to assist them more promptly and productively.

Try this: picture the beliefs someone needs to buy from you as a chain. Each belief is linked to (or chained to) another belief. This chain extends from where your prospect is now all the way to your product.

We call this chain the *chain of beliefs*.

The Chain of Beliefs

Back to my beer brewing courses, I once hosted a livestream for my audience. During the livestream, I kept saying a particular brewing term. At one point, I glanced at the monitor and saw blank stares.

"Wait, do you guys even know what this term means?" I asked them.

A few shook their heads, confessing their lack of knowledge. I could see most of the others felt the same. I saw my error: I had made an incorrect assumption about what my audience knew.

"Okay, let's start at the beginning," I told them.

This story is a microcosm of what happens every day when prospective customers read marketing material published by businesses. When you're publishing emails, blogs, or PDFs, you're not present in the room to see those heads shaking. You don't have the opportunity to hear your prospects say, "I have no clue what you're talking about."

You often never even consider that your reader doesn't share your assumptions, because they don't have your knowledge.

Imagine a prospect trying to read your sales page without even the basic understanding to make sense of it. They don't buy, so you decide to lower the price. But if the prospect doesn't understand what you're offering, the price isn't the issue. Not yet, at least.

I recommend stepping into your customers' shoes and imagining what it's like to see the world through the lens of their current knowledge and beliefs. Only then will you be able to publish messaging that aligns with those beliefs and takes your prospect step-by-step along the path to new beliefs, resulting in them buying your product.

I first heard the term chain of beliefs from my friend and colleague, Rich Schefren, a brilliant marketer who has a deep understanding of human psychology.

You might have heard of this concept, also called the sequence of beliefs or the chain of agreements. These names all refer to the same concept: the path your prospect takes from not knowing anything about you or your topic to becoming a loyal customer.

You create your chain of beliefs when you link together all the beliefs your prospects need to go from unaware to fully informed. Your goal is to fix any broken links and form a strong chain that gives your prospect a direct path to your product.

When you have a strong, solid chain of beliefs, your prospect will proceed through that chain until they reach the last belief, the one where they ultimately say, "Yes, this product is worth my money. I will buy it."

In the next chapter, you'll get an exercise that helps you identify the required beliefs for your product or service.

For now, let's use a visual to see how the chain of beliefs works.

Imagine your marketing efforts as occurring inside concentric rings. You, the seller, are broadcasting your messaging out from the center.

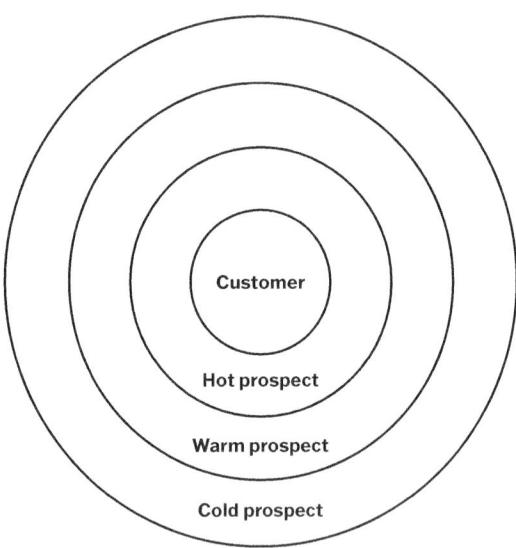

These concentric circles show how receptive prospects are
to your offering based on their current level of belief.

Your easiest-to-convert prospects will be those in the inner rings. Those prospects are the people who already hold most of the beliefs needed to buy your product.

They understand they have a problem, are familiar with the different approaches available, which includes your approach, and they're familiar with you and your company, too.

Additionally, these inner-ring prospects don't have false beliefs or false assumptions that block them from fully valuing your offer. With these prospects, you don't have to do a ton of educating before they "get it."

The beliefs you'll need to instill in these prospects are more related to your offer. You'll need to instill beliefs about how your product will work for them, how you deliver your offering, and if now is a good time for them to purchase.

Ideally, it would be great to have a bottomless well of these prospects that never runs dry. Unfortunately, you'll eventually exhaust this group.

You may have had this experience when you've launched a product and your loyal fans buy instantly. But then, after that honeymoon phase is over, you find it harder to convert new customers.

What happened? You exhausted your well of true believers. The good news? You can refill the well. You do so by venturing to the outer rings.

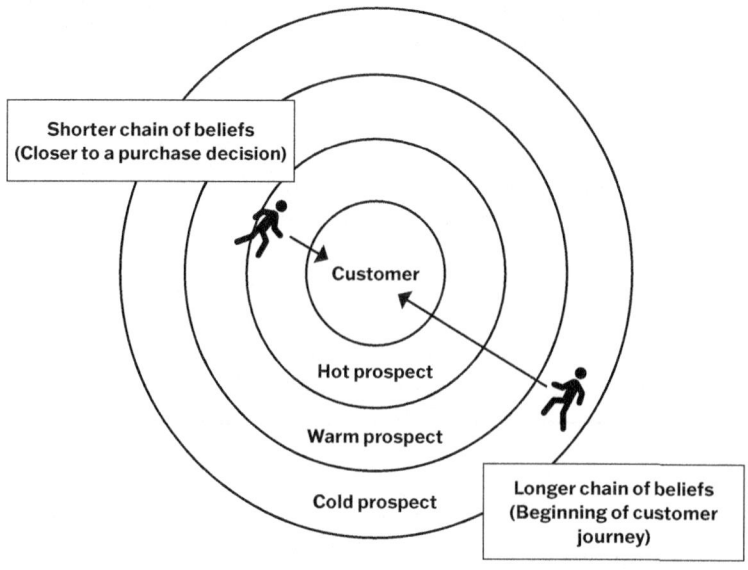

Some prospects require more Belief Building than others. To win a customer, your marketing content must bring prospects from the outer rings into the inner rings, where they will be most receptive to your offering

In the outer rings, you will find millions more people. And through your marketing content, you can guide these people down the chain of beliefs into the inner ring.

To do so, you'll need to meet those prospects where they are. And make no mistake, these are not inner-ring prospects—you'll need to communicate with them in a different way.

Have you ever met with a prospect, and after a minute of talking you realize this person has no clue about your field? You realize your conversation is going to take far longer than expected, and you'll need an hour to simply get them up to speed. Forget about discussing your offering—that'll be down the road, if you can even get there.

In this scenario, it's clear you're talking to outer-ring prospects who have a long chain of beliefs.

In order to turn these outer-ring prospects into inner-ring prospects, you must educate them. Only once they're up to speed does it make sense to present your offering.

You can educate them in a one-on-one sales conversation, of course, but that's not very time-efficient or scalable. No, this isn't a job for sales, but one for marketing.

Specifically, this is a job for your marketing *content*. Your marketing content stems from your core message and flows down channels like your website, emails, blog posts, and ads. It's through these channels that your marketing content educates and informs your prospects.

Would you rather talk to 10,000 people one-on-one or send out a piece of marketing material that reaches 10,000 people all at once? Marketing content gives you the ability to multiply yourself so your message can reach thousands or even millions of prospects.

Within that marketing material, you'll employ Belief Building.

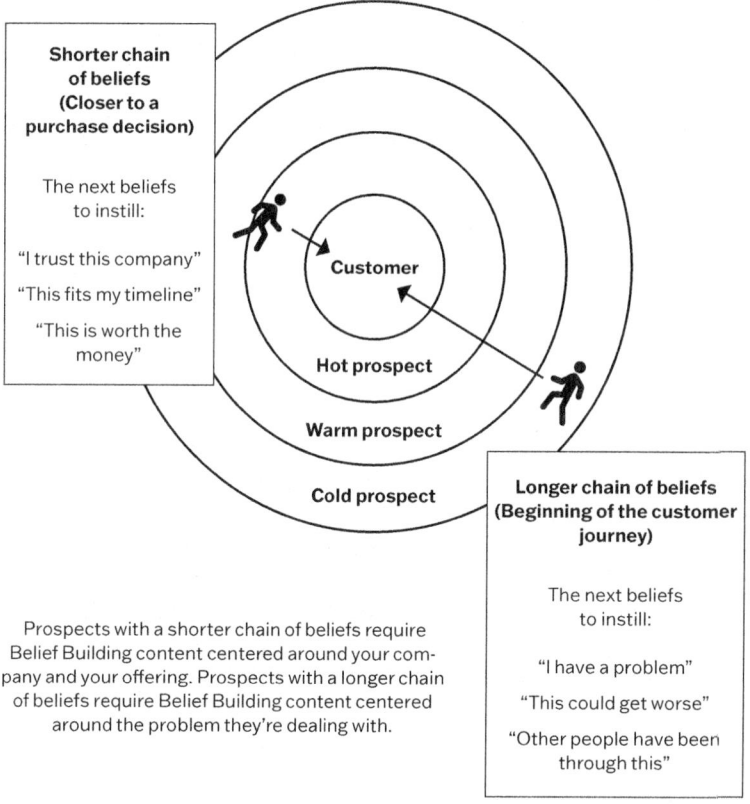

Shorter chain of beliefs (Closer to a purchase decision)

The next beliefs to instill:

"I trust this company"

"This fits my timeline"

"This is worth the money"

Customer

Hot prospect

Warm prospect

Cold prospect

Longer chain of beliefs (Beginning of the customer journey)

The next beliefs to instill:

"I have a problem"

"This could get worse"

"Other people have been through this"

Prospects with a shorter chain of beliefs require Belief Building content centered around your company and your offering. Prospects with a longer chain of beliefs require Belief Building content centered around the problem they're dealing with.

You can see how the prospects who are closer to the center have a shorter chain of beliefs. Mentally, they're most of the way toward seeing the value in your offer. They're aware of their problem, they know the landscape of solutions, they know what to look for, and they are simply searching for the best provider.

Prospects in the outer rings have a longer chain of beliefs. They're not even aware of their problem yet, know nothing about your area of expertise, and have many incorrect assumptions.

Prospects with a Longer Chain of Beliefs
- Don't recognize they have a problem.
- Don't know about potential solutions.
- Don't know your topic.
- Don't know you.

Prospect with a Shorter Chain of Beliefs
- Don't know if your offer is a good value.
- Don't know if now is a good time to buy.
- Don't know if your product will be easy to use.
- Don't know if they should trust you.

Do you see why these two different prospects require different messaging?

Using the same messaging for each prospect would lead to confusion and frustration, and ultimately hurt your sales. Belief Building allows you to tailor your messaging to each prospect's current beliefs.

This "tailor the message to the prospect's beliefs" approach is supported by the principles of effective copywriting. Copywriters know that warm prospects respond best to messaging that focuses on price, the guarantee, and the trustworthiness of the company.

On the other hand, cold prospects aren't ready for direct offers. They need messaging that first addresses the problem, introduces the solutions, and finally, presents your solution.

Right now, consider who you are currently reaching with your marketing. Are you speaking to prospects with a shorter chain of beliefs, or longer?

Your best bet is to start by targeting prospects in the inner rings, the ones with the shorter chain of beliefs. These prospects require less education, and it will be less work to convert them into customers.

Convert that low-hanging fruit, build up your cash reserves, and then make your advancement into the outer rings. This "Normandy Strategy" of taking one beach at a time allows you to fund your expansion efforts by first securing the easy sales.

Be forewarned: you'll quickly exhaust the pool of true believers. Once you do, you'll need to venture into the outer rings, which requires educating colder prospects. That takes time, money, and effort, but the potential in reaching so many new people makes it worthwhile.

In business, you need to manage your resources wisely, and this situation is no different. You've got to strike a balance.

Today, should you venture out and try to reach colder prospects? Or do you have more gold to mine with your current audience? This is a question every business owner must wrestle with.

Here's some guidance:

Buyers tend to be repeat buyers. Surprisingly, people who have purchased products similar to yours are often the most likely to buy your product next. It may seem counterintuitive, as you might assume that once someone has bought a certain kind of product, they're less likely to buy again.

However, research consistently shows that your best prospects are often your existing customers. This can be attributed to various factors, such as loyalty and familiarity with your company. But there's another reason: your existing customers already hold the beliefs needed to make a purchase.

Similarly, customers of other companies selling products like yours are likely to hold those required beliefs, and for you, this translates into a promising pool of prospects.

When targeting customers of companies similar to yours, your task is to instill beliefs around how your product is different. This is a distinct challenge from instilling beliefs around the problem—your competitors' customers are past that stage. They know their problem.

So, one great way to decide who to target first with your marketing message is to start with customers who have bought products or services similar to yours.

After that, experiment with broader audiences and gauge the response. We find that when we expand the scope of our content and dedicate messaging to more foundational beliefs, we discover a few key beliefs we'd been taking for granted. This revelation often serves as a wake-up call for our audience. They begin to buzz about our new content, clicking on emails, sharing the material, and making purchases.

It's a clear indication that we've struck a nerve.

I had this happen with a North Carolina–based online education company that sold self-improvement programs. They had been in business for forty years, had a loyal audience, a huge email list, and posted to their Facebook page multiple times per day.

But when I looked at their product line, I couldn't find a good on-ramp into learning their topic. I was lost and confused.

After being in business for forty years, they became too close to their products. They forgot what it's like to be a beginner. They failed to see their products with fresh eyes and, as a result, they took many beliefs for granted.

This company threw terms around casually. They didn't provide any links back to foundational ideas, and new subscribers were thrown straight into the deep end.

My research confirmed that many people in their audience, like me, were confused by the concepts and terms in the company's marketing material.

We tested my assumption by launching a new online course. I made its topic extremely basic and introductory. My client was confused.

"It's too simple," they said. "Our audience is more advanced."

(Not the first time I've heard that.)

But my client trusted me, and we launched the online course. A few weeks later, after the launch ended, the company's president sent me an email:

This course launch was our largest revenue event in our company's forty-year history. Thank you.

My client had woken up to how few people in their audience held the beliefs required to fully value their products. They finally understood why none of the coupons they handed out had the desired effect.

My client assumed people weren't buying because their prices were too high. I showed them that people weren't buying because my client had taken their prospects' beliefs for granted.

Once we educated their prospects and got everyone up to speed, people started buying. And not just that introductory course, either. Sales picked up for all the other products, too.

This makes sense because these customers, after being more educated on my client's topic, could now fully appreciate their advanced offerings.

In the end, our Belief Building efforts led to a domino effect that lifted product sales across the board. This effect is common when you effectively apply Belief Building.

Now, was there a drawback for my client? Yes.

My client had to invest resources into this effort. They had to transition their team onto this project, pause other efforts, and pay me for consulting.

This is the balancing act I previously mentioned. When you decide to expand into those outer rings to reach colder prospects (belief-wise), it's not free, so you must decide if it's worth it. For my client it was.

No, this game isn't always easy. But now that you understand Belief Building, you know which game you're playing. Now, let's help you master the game.

Three Methods to Identify Your Prospect's Current Beliefs

You know the importance of your prospect's current beliefs, but how do you identify them?

Method 1: Listen for the (Bad) Questions Your Customer Asks

One method to uncover what your prospects currently believe is to listen closely to the questions they ask you. The most useful questions are what you might call "wrong" or "bad" or even "dumb" questions (although I hope you keep these thoughts to yourself).

You know your topic inside and out—but not everyone does. When these less-experienced people ask questions about your topic, do they ever ask the wrong question?

I always found the answer to be yes.

When I was teaching beer brewing, I'd often get asked questions from beginners that were far too advanced. Let's do a quick beer brewing lesson.

Beer has four ingredients: water, malt, hops, and yeast. Most people know that yeast creates alcohol, but few know that yeast also contributes significantly to the beer's flavor.

Yeast strains are regional. It's similar to winemaking, where grapes are regional. A beer made with American yeast will taste different than a beer made with British yeast.

Follow me so far?

When a new brewer asks, "Which yeast should I use, American or Belgian?" that's not a bad question—yet.

However, I'd often get far more in-the-weeds questions like, "Which yeast strain should I use, northern Belgian or southern Belgian?"

That is a bad question for a new brewer to be asking. It's far too nuanced, and only an advanced brewer should worry about it at all.

In fact, it would be detrimental for me to answer that question. Answering that question implicitly tells them, "That's a good question to ask."

When a new brewer asks this question, I respond, "I hear you, and I understand why you want to know that, but let me share something I wish I knew when I first got started . . ."

Next, I'll ask them about their current brewing practices, what steps they are taking, and the results they're getting. That allows me to give them a better question to ask.

That's a key point to highlight: **give your prospects better questions to ask**.

(Also, handle this situation delicately without embarrassing the person. It takes courage for a beginner to ask an expert a question.)

In teaching homebrewing, I learned that many home brewers were not properly cleaning and sanitizing their equipment.

Homebrewed beer is highly vulnerable to infection, and improper cleaning and sanitization are the leading cause of bad flavors. And isn't that ultimately the home brewer's goal? To brew good-tasting beer?

This new home brewer simply assumed—due to their inexperience—that their original question about the yeast was the best way to achieve that goal. So, by rejecting that initial "wrong" question, you're not doing anything unkind. Quite the opposite. You're showing them how to get what they want—by showing them a better way.

Think about your audience. What do they really want? What questions do they ask that aren't the best questions for achieving that goal? How can you redirect them and show them a better path?

The next time you talk to a prospect or client, listen closely to the questions they ask. It will clue you in to their current beliefs and what they think is important.

You'll get a tool in the next chapter that will help you more with redirecting questions to focus on what's most important.

For now, let's move on to the second method for discovering current beliefs.

Method 2: Ask *Them* Questions

The key is to create a space where your customer feels comfortable sharing. They shouldn't feel judged or pressured. Here is a methodology you can follow.

What/How Questions

You'll hear many approaches to customer research that teach you to ask a bunch of "why" questions, digging deeper each time. You'll sometimes hear this referred to as "The Five Whys."

Why did you do that?
And why did you do that?
Why is that?
But why?
Why?

And so on.

I recommend you avoid these questions.

Tiago and I have a common mentor, Joe Hudson, who taught us a better technique. Joe is a top executive coach and the best I've seen when it comes to deeply empathizing with a person.[1]

Joe points out that "why" questions often appear judgmental and make people defensive, which prevents them from sharing their genuine feelings.

Instead, Joe recommends using "what" and "how" questions. These tend to be softer and, as a result, lead to the person being more forthcoming.

For example, instead of asking, "Why did you do that?" your question becomes, "What were you trying to accomplish?" or "How did you go about making that decision?"

Do you see how these questions are not only gentler, but also make it easier for the person to answer?

---

1   You can learn more about Joe Hudson and his business Art of Accomplishment through the website https://www.artofaccomplishment.com/.

Here are some other questions you might ask:

1. What led you to purchase X product or hire X service provider?
2. Think about the last time this problem occurred. How did you deal with it?
3. What makes it important for you to succeed with X?

For example, for Joe's executive coaching business, he might ask a CEO, "What makes it important for you to be seen as a strong leader?" as opposed to, "Why is it important for you to be seen as a stronger leader?"

Use these what/how questions—they work wonders.

Method 3: Peek into the Cycles of Your Prospect's Life

Most of those common "define your ideal customer" exercises aren't very helpful. Have you ever noticed that?

You know the drill . . .

"My customer is Sophie, she's 35, she drives a black 4Runner, she makes $80K per year."

That demographic information can be helpful, but it does little to uncover your prospect's *beliefs*, which is what we're after.

Let me give you a better tool for customer research: the Cycles-Based Approach.

It's overwhelming to try and understand *everything* about a customer's life. Fortunately for those of us tasked with marketing duties, humans live their lives in cycles. You might also call these rituals, routines, or patterns.

In our marketing efforts, we can tap into these cycles. In doing so, we can uncover our prospect's beliefs.

Example: Physical Therapist

For example, if you're a physical therapist, you know that a person becoming injured unfolds as a cycle. There's a pattern of what happens before the injury, during the injury, and after. If you're a physical therapist and you are investigating your client's cycles, you might ask, "What does a person do when they become injured? What is the pattern of behavior?"

If you're that physical therapist treating a patient, after ensuring your patient is comfortable and open to discussion, to find this cycle, you could ask them to describe what happened.

"Can you walk me through what happened when you got injured?"

Your patient responds, "Well, I was playing soccer, and I twisted my ankle. It hurt a lot, but I didn't want to seem weak in front of my team, so I tried to play through the pain. It became unbearable, and I had to stop. I rested for a couple of days, took some over-the-counter painkillers, and used ice packs. I didn't see a doctor until a week later when the pain and swelling didn't improve."

If you're the physical therapist, you instantly recognize this cycle. And you also notice certain beliefs. Let's examine them.

Pride: The patient didn't want to seem weak, indicating a belief in maintaining a certain image among peers, even at the risk of worsening the injury.

Self-Reliance: Initially, the patient tried home remedies, showing a tendency to avoid professional help, perhaps due to a belief that the injury wasn't severe enough to seek medical attention, or to save costs.

Influence of Past Experiences: If the patient has a pattern of trying self-care before visiting a professional, it may tell you their beliefs have been influenced by past experiences, possibly where self-care solved the problem—or a professional didn't.

These insights are gold.

Armed with this information, the physical therapist can tailor their approach and communication to better resonate with their patient's beliefs.

Do you see how when we identified the cycle, we identified the beliefs?

Let's do another example, so you really get the hang of it.

Example: Leadership Coach

My client, Clarke Ching, is known as "The Bottleneck Guy." Corporations hire Clarke to coach their senior leaders through a very demanding cycle. This cycle occurs when a company releases a hit new product and demand soars.

At first, Clarke's client is happy. After all, soaring product demand is good news. But then reality sets in. When product demand soars, the company must hire a slew of people to keep up. And who is responsible for all of these new people? Clarke's client, the senior leader.

Suddenly, they're doing the job of two or three people. They struggle to keep up. With all these new employees, they're so busy managing, they don't have time to lead.

As a result, Clarke's client becomes the bottleneck in the company. The problem is, they don't realize they're the bottleneck (or don't want to admit it).

Clarke has witnessed this cycle many times, and can predict the pattern of behavior. In response to the spike in workload, the senior leader will:

- Read books on time management.
- Take productivity courses.
- Work late into the evening, taking pride in "being the hero."
- Furiously update the task management software last thing at night, first thing in the morning.
- Micromanage their employees.

From these behaviors, we can learn much about the senior manager's current beliefs, such as:

- The problem is my time management.
- I'm not the bottleneck, I'm just very busy.
- If I take a break, everything will break.
- It's easier if I do it myself.

If Clarke fails to acknowledge these beliefs and jumps right into his solution, he'll never obtain the buy-in he needs from his client to create true transformation and get them back to being a leader.

Before presenting his solution, Clarke must meet his client where they are. The senior leader must feel seen and heard. Once that occurs, Clarke can better help them understand the true cause of their problem. And then, finally, he can introduce his solution.

Once again, when you peek into the cycles of your customer's life and witness how they behave, you can better understand their current beliefs. Only then can you create a lasting transformation.

That is why this cycle-based approach is one of my favorite tools for market research. Give it a shot and you'll love it, too.

No matter which research method you choose:

- Study your prospects to find patterns, commonalities, and prevalent beliefs.

- Look for insights that challenge your assumptions. Did you find any surprises?
- Spot anything you've been assuming in your marketing material that just isn't true. Have you been taking a belief for granted? Do you need to back up a step and address a belief that's further up the chain of beliefs?

This exercise tends to highlight the smart person's curse of knowledge. It shows where you've been assuming your prospect knows or believes something—but your assumption has been mistaken.

Congrats. Equipped with your new insights, you're now better able to align your offerings with your customers' beliefs and desires.

Now that you have an understanding of your prospects' current beliefs, it's time for your next step: determine the beliefs your prospects need in order to be pre-sold on your offer.

CHAPTER SEVEN

Identifying Your Customer's Required Beliefs

By BILLY BROAS

"Meet your prospect where they are."

You've likely heard this timeless marketing advice before, but what does it mean? Belief Building sheds new light on this old adage.

With Belief Building, we establish a shared reality between you and your prospect. It's much like making a logical argument.

Imagine placing an apple on a table between you and your prospect. You both acknowledge it's there—one apple, undeniable and clear. This agreement is your starting point, the shared reality from which all further discussions with your prospect unfold.

In marketing, identifying this "apple"—the undeniable truth that both you and your prospect can agree upon—sets the stage for everything that follows.

Belief Building operates on this principle. It constructs a pathway from your shared reality to new beliefs about your topic and, ultimately, your product. Each step forward requires mutual understanding.

If one person insists there are two apples on the table when there's clearly just one, the conversation has nowhere to go. There's no shared agreement to build upon.

By establishing a common ground, Belief Building ensures both you and your prospect are on the same page, ready to explore new ideas together.

But here's where the subtlety of marketing comes into play. Just as you wouldn't start a logical argument with a premise your audience disputes, you shouldn't begin your marketing efforts from a point of disagreement or misunderstanding.

Instead, start where agreement is easy, then build your case, introducing new beliefs and reinforcing them until the value of your offering becomes self-evident.

This chapter dives into how you can systematically identify shared truths with your audience and use them as stepping stones. By carefully guiding your prospects from simple, undeniable agreements, you lead them to the logical conclusion that your product or service is not just a good choice—but the inevitable one.

This method doesn't manipulate or coerce. Instead, we turn prospects into informed, confident customers who know they've arrived at the purchase decision through their own logic and reasoning.

Are you seeing how marketing is more than hashtags and hype?

Let's return to our focusing question: What does my prospect need to believe in order to buy?

How do we answer that question?

For years, I did it this way. "Hmm . . . Well, my customer needs to believe this. Oh, and this, too. And *this* and *this*."

But then I'd hit a wall. After doing this exercise many times, I realized I needed a road map to identify the required beliefs.

Scratching my head, I asked myself, "Could there be categories or perhaps stages of belief?"

I glanced at my desk and saw a sketch I had made for a marketing campaign I was working on. The sketch showed the path those customers would take to buying the product.

In a lightbulb moment, it dawned on me: the good ol' customer journey. That was the answer.

Anchor Beliefs to the Customer Journey

Everything clicked when I mapped the essential beliefs our prospects needed directly onto the stages of their journey to our product.

But first, what is the customer journey?

Think of it like building a romantic relationship, where someone goes through a series of considerations and milestones before committing. Rushing from first awareness to final decision rarely turns out well.

Additionally, the products or services you're selling are likely not impulse buys. That means you need to think about how your prospect's journey unfolds over time, whether that is one week later or one year down the road.

Now, let's break down this journey into its critical stages:

1. Awareness
2. Consideration
3. Decision

Let's examine each stage, and then we'll see how we can anchor our required beliefs to them.

Awareness

In the awareness stage, customers realize there is a problem. They are no longer happy with the status quo and are looking to end their feelings of frustration.

The customer is looking for acknowledgment that your business understands their problem. Your marketing content should elicit the reaction, "Wow, this business really gets me."

The beliefs you instill here should help the customer learn more about their problem. At this stage, they can't fully articulate it.

If you can come along and give them the words to better describe their problem, you'll not only elicit that, "Wow, they get me," reaction, but also, "Maybe this person can help me."

Consideration

In the consideration stage, the customer is exploring—or considering—potential solutions. When you want to solve a problem, you have options to choose from. Some are more direct and some are outside the box.

The beliefs you build at this stage will position your product as a viable solution. You're tossing your hat in the ring and saying, "We can help you, too."

At the same time, the beliefs you instill should invalidate the other options. We want there to be just one option: you.

Decision

This stage is where the exchange of cash for your product or service takes place. It's here the transition from marketing to selling occurs. If you've effectively executed your marketing, the selling process should be much smoother.

Rather than forcefully persuading your prospect, you'll simply open the door, allowing them to confidently step through.

It's a common pitfall, however, for smart people to excel in marketing yet stumble in the selling phase. Don't falter at the finish line! In this crucial stage, it's essential to reinforce the belief in your trustworthiness and assure the customer they're making the right decision.

When we map out the customer journey, we clarify the beliefs needed for a purchase. By imposing constraints, we leverage your analytical mind. We began with our key question, "What does the customer need to believe in order to buy?"

This question narrows down the vast array of marketing tasks to a singular focus. But we can refine it further. By dividing the question into three distinct phases—awareness, consideration, and decision—we apply targeted constraints to each stage of the customer journey.

Do you see how this makes marketing more like a puzzle to solve? And puzzles are far easier to solve when you have the pieces.

To help you drill down even more, we've developed customized Belief Building questions for each stage of the customer journey. Use these questions to kickstart your efforts in identifying the beliefs your prospects need to have in order to buy from you.

Belief Building: Questions to Ask to Identify the Beliefs Your Prospect Needs in Order to Buy

What does my customer need to believe in the Awareness stage?
1. What do they need to believe about their problem?
2. What do they need to believe about the prevalence of their problem?

3. What do they need to believe about what happens if the problem doesn't get solved?

What does my customer need to believe in the Consideration stage?
1. What do they need to believe about their different options?
2. What do they need to believe about my option?
3. What do they need to believe about the risks associated with inaction?

What does my customer need to believe in the Decision stage?
1. What do they need to believe about me?
2. What do they need to believe about my product?
3. What do they need to believe about what happens after purchase?

Set aside time to go through these questions. Bring in your business partners, employees, colleagues, or collaborators to provide their perspectives. They can often help the business owner notice something they've missed. Every perspective helps, and the more people you involve in brainstorming your prospect's required beliefs, the better.

Challenge yourself to dig deep, too. There are always beliefs located beneath the surface that won't be immediately apparent. Remember Tiago and the belief that caught him blindsided?

That belief came from a group of academics who took his online course, *Building a Second Brain*. The academics had the false belief that Tiago's note-taking system promoted plagiarism.

Where would that belief fall in the questions above? In the consideration stage: What do they need to believe about my option?

In Tiago's case, his customers need to believe his option will solve their problem of drowning in information overwhelm. Tiago says, "Hey, I have an option to help you solve that problem. It involves digital note-taking."

Now, this is important . . .

Whenever you recommend your option, there will always be objections. Even if your prospect is excited and hopeful about your option, they will still have objections.

"Will this work for me?"

"What if I'm a beginner?"

"What if I don't live in the United States?"

And so on.

In Tiago's situation, the objection was: This option promotes plagiarism. Tiago had to:

1. Recognize the objection.
2. Overcome the objection.

Because he was so close to his product, Tiago had a blind spot to this objection.

You have blind spots too. We all do. That's why it's important to bring others into this exercise. Much of my work as a consultant is uncovering my client's blind spots.

Now, let me give you a handy tool to help you identify your prospect's required beliefs.

The Ladder of Importance

When it comes to having success in your field, have some factors been more important than others?

I'm sure if we examined your career path, some actions you've taken have made a massive difference, while other actions . . . not so much.

For the actions, attitudes, and behaviors that made a difference to your success, let's call these your "success factors."

Next, visualize these success factors as a hierarchy, with the most important factors at the top and the less important factors at the bottom. We'll visualize this hierarchy as a ladder. You might think of it as a "success ladder."

Let's look at an example from the field of photography.

When I was consulting with an online photography teacher, his audience believed there was a dominant success factor: the quality of the camera. In order for my client to get more customers, we had to dethrone that belief from the top of the success factors hierarchy, or what we'll from now on call the Ladder of Importance.

In photography, the amount of money you spend on the camera is *not* the most important factor. The most important factors have to do with the skill of the photographer.

When it comes to taking great photos, the Ladder of Importance may look like this:

Ladder of Importance for Photography

The key success factors for taking great photos. A photography teacher should teach what's important before teaching implementation details.

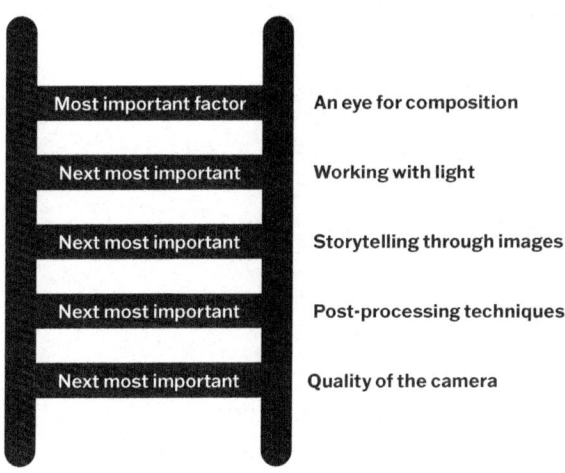

Most important factor	**An eye for composition**
Next most important	**Working with light**
Next most important	**Storytelling through images**
Next most important	**Post-processing techniques**
Next most important	**Quality of the camera**

What happens if the beginner photographer believes the quality of the camera is the first rung? How receptive will that student be to a new online course called, *How to Develop an Eye for Composition*?

It's your job to make sure your prospect's Ladder of Importance matches yours. And you do this through your marketing content and the Belief Building process.

Let's look at more example using the beer brewing scenario from the last chapter.

Remember, my students were asking me detailed questions about yeast strains. At the same time, they weren't properly cleaning and sanitizing their equipment, which is far more important.

Thus, my Ladder of Importance for beer brewing looks like this.

Ladder of Importance for Brewing Beer

The key success factors for brewing great tasting beer.

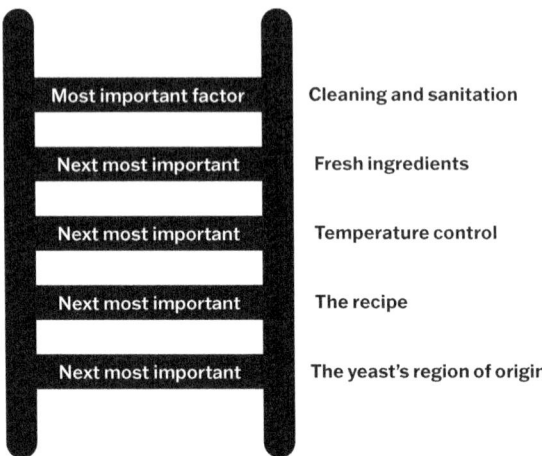

Most important factor	Cleaning and sanitation
Next most important	Fresh ingredients
Next most important	Temperature control
Next most important	The recipe
Next most important	The yeast's region of origin

If I'm speaking to a new brewer, I tell them to put the most attention on that top rung of the ladder—cleaning and sanitizing.

"Cleaning and sanitizing is more important," is how I would phrase it. Notice how this phrasing ties back to the Ladder of Importance. I'm making an argument for what's important—the top rung of the ladder.

The Ladder of Importance will help you combat the curse of knowledge. It will help you surface what you've been taking for granted. Too many smart people are out there teaching detailed tutorials on extremely niche questions instead of teaching what's fundamentally important.

An answer to the question, "What's important?" is what your customers really want to know from you. The implementation details can come later. If you were new to a topic, wouldn't you want the same?

Take a few minutes and sketch out your Ladder of Importance. You'll find your ladder most useful when creating content for the Consideration phase, where you are presenting the argument for your recommended way of doing things.

The Ladder of Importance for [Your Topic]

Top Rung: ___[Success Factor]___
Second Rung: ___[Success Factor]___
Third Rung: ___[Success Factor]___
Fourth Rung: ___[Success Factor]___
Fifth Rung: ___[Success Factor]___

And so on.

The Changing Landscape of Beliefs

Remember, the notes you're taking and the beliefs you're writing down are a living, breathing document.

You'll need to keep revising these beliefs. Every time a new competitor gains traction, or a popular new product captures your audience's attention, or there's a new technological breakthrough in your field, you'll need to revisit and update your list of required beliefs.

For example, when AI began taking off in 2023, it became a new solution for customers' problems. It became a new option for Consideration, to use our customer journey terminology.

Because of the rise of AI, business owners everywhere were forced to address this new option. If a business pretended as though AI didn't exist, that business came off as out of touch.

No, that doesn't mean every business needs to adopt AI or become AI experts, but all businesses should have conveyed to their customers how AI was impacting them—if at all. You can bet their competitors were talking about AI.

And who is the customer more likely to listen to? The business that's current with the times, or the one that doesn't seem to be paying attention?

This process of identifying new beliefs is never-ending, because the world keeps spinning and the competitive landscape keeps evolving. Competitors enter and leave, customer desires change, and trends emerge. Your business and products change, too.

Those changes must be communicated. False beliefs must be cleared away and new beliefs must be instilled. That's how you stay relevant and competitive in your industry.

Now, let's get into the *instill* part of the Belief Building process.

Here, we'll switch from knowing the required beliefs—to communicating them.

CHAPTER EIGHT

Build Belief Part 1

By BILLY BROAS

Did the Ladder of Importance give you new ideas on what you could be saying in your marketing content? The exercise often has that effect.

That's because it highlights the assumptions a business owner has been making about their topic and prospect. They've been taking rungs on the ladder for granted.

You can now see why, without Belief Building, giving discounts often fails to convert as many customers as we might expect, and shrinks profits too. Without the beliefs needed to buy, without knowing what's important (and what's not), your prospects will resist any offer you make—even if you offer a discount.

We would, of course, prefer to both gain customers *and* maintain healthy profit margins.

Belief Building will give you both. To recap, in our Belief Building process, you:

1. Identified your prospect's current beliefs.
2. Identified the beliefs your prospect needs in order to buy.
3. Organized and prioritized those required beliefs.

Congrats, because by this point, you've already empathized with your prospects more than most businesses ever will.

I can't tell you how many businesses I've come across that are obsessed with their website design, the latest software, and their sales funnels, yet they take virtually zero time to put themselves in their customer's shoes and walk that person's journey from start to finish.

When you walk that journey, identifying each of their needed beliefs, you realize how much you've been assuming, and why your prospects might be confused or even frustrated.

Rest assured, when you start giving voice to the beliefs you've been taking for granted and begin educating your prospects, you'll see an immediate uptick in response.

Your audience will click more, reply more, and buy more. All because you met them where they were and led them by the hand to the best solution for them.

It's a win-win.

You now have a bevy of beliefs written down, but how do you bridge the gap between your prospect's required beliefs and your finished marketing content?

How do we turn your list of required beliefs into a website, emails, a webinar, and more?

We begin by telling you the goal of your marketing efforts. Many people fail to realize what they're actually supposed to do when they sit down to do marketing.

You're Making an Argument

Don't think about what you're doing as marketing—think about it as making an argument.

You're making an argument for your way of doing things. You're arguing for why some factors are more important than others. Think back to our photography example.

Imagine I'm a photography teacher and I tell a student, "The most important thing in photography is developing an eye for composition."

Should that student automatically believe me? No way. I need to argue the case that developing an eye for composition is the most important success factor in photography.

In your marketing, you're making an argument. That's your job.

No, not *that* type of argument. Not a "throw your phone against the wall" sort of argument. Not an emotional confrontation. We're talking a *rhetorical argument.*

In our modern world, with all our marketing technology, we've forgotten where marketing comes from: the field of rhetoric. Rhetoric is the art of persuasive communication and dates back to the ancient Greeks. Aristotle is primarily credited with developing the basics of rhetoric back in the fourth century BC.

Rhetoric is everywhere. You use it every day when you:

- Convince your friends to go to the new restaurant in town.
- Explain to your daughter why certain rules exist in the home.
- Argue your point in a book club discussion.

Wouldn't it be helpful for everyone to learn the basics for something we use so often and with so much at stake?

But it's even more important for you. If you're tasked with marketing yourself, then learning even the basics of rhetoric will pay immediate dividends anytime you talk about what you do for a living.

I'll show you an example of rhetoric using a familiar scenario. Then, I'll show you how we employ rhetoric in the Belief Building process.

Think of Those Courtroom Dramas

Let's pretend you're a lawyer in a courtroom. You're defending your client, Jimmy, who was recently caught shoplifting. You're pleading for the judge to go light on Jimmy.

You address the court. "Your honor, I'd like to show you that my client Jimmy is trying to turn his life around."

That's the belief you need the judge to mentally accept: Jimmy is turning his life around.

If you persuade the judge, she may go easy on Jimmy.

Would this argument be effective if all you said was, "Jimmy is trying to turn his life around," and were finished? Nope.

The judge, peeved about Jimmy's offence, thinks, "I don't believe you."

Remember, we need the judge's mental acceptance that our statement, "Jimmy is turning his life around," is true.

Do you recognize that type of statement? It's a *claim*. And what must follow a claim? From the field of rhetoric, we know what must follow a claim is *proof*.

Yes, you must provide proof to support your claims, whether you're speaking to a judge, to an audience from a conference stage, or on your landing page.

In our courtroom example, should we rely on a *single* form of proof? No way.

Again, go back to those courtroom dramas. What do you see?

"Your honor, I present Exhibit A."

Then Exhibit B, Exhibit C, and so on.

A lawyer in a courtroom presents a lot of different pieces of evidence, each contributing to prove their claim. With each piece of evidence, the lawyer's case gets stronger and stronger. It's often the cumulative evidence that sways a judge or jury.

Approach your marketing the same way. Be that lawyer in the courtroom. When you're creating your marketing content, add evidence upon evidence; make the case for buying your product stronger and stronger. Back up your claims with proof until your argument is airtight.

Let's try it now with Jimmy.

Exercise: Come up with proof to back up the claim that Jimmy is trying to turn his life around.

Still pretending to be Jimmy's lawyer, let's come up with three forms of proof (a.k.a. evidence) to back up our claim: Jimmy is turning his life around.

Stop here and brainstorm a few proof examples. This exercise will give you valuable practice for applying this technique to your marketing efforts.

___[Form of proof]___
___[Form of proof]___
___[Form of proof]___

How did it go? Come up with any?

Here are a few pieces of proof I came up with:

1. An exam paper from Jimmy's community college with an "A" written on it.
2. The leader of the volunteer shelter where Jimmy works praising him.
3. A story about Jimmy's harsh upbringing and abusive parents. This proof point helps the judge empathize with Jimmy and have a better understanding of why he may be misbehaving.

What do you think? Do you think after seeing this evidence, our judge is even 1% more likely to reduce Jimmy's punishment? I believe so.

The Real Task of the Marketer

Few realize that the primary job of marketing content is to make an argument. Most business owners recognize the importance of content creation, yet they often fall into the trap of a topic-based approach.

This common strategy involves publishing content broadly related to their topic of expertise—whether it's beer brewing, photography, productivity, or any other field. You can't blame them. It's a natural inclination and is reinforced by countless "experts" who advise, "Keep publishing content around your topic, and then delve into its subtopics!"

I, too, followed the topic-based approach, exhausting myself with free content. It gained me likes and followers, but not many sales. It wasn't until I studied the great copywriters that I realized I had been taking a topic-based approach, when I should have been taking an argument-based approach.

Once I switched to making an argument, my sales increased. More surprisingly, my readers actually preferred this new method. Before, when I posted about my topic, I'd receive polite thank-yous and nods of appreciation. But when I began to assert my claims, the responses deepened and became more heartfelt. It was clear I was delivering greater value to my audience.

The argument-based approach also boosted my confidence—a change my audience noticed. They were looking for more than information. They wanted guidance from someone willing to take a stand, and constructing content as an argument for a particular viewpoint does more than share information—it creates clarity and conviction.

The success of the argument-based approach isn't just anecdotal. It's backed by research on effective communication. One study taught a technical subject to two groups using the two different methods. The first group was taught using a conventional topic-based approach. The presenter shared slides full of bullet points and graphics that explained the topic, but didn't take a stand. The second group learned through slides that presented assertions backed by evidence.[1]

The results were telling—those who learned through the assertion-based slides had a statistically significant better understanding and retention of the material. This demonstrates that presenting your case with conviction and evidence not only resonates more, but also has a lasting impact on your audience's memory.

Have you been merely publishing content related to your topic, or have you been making an argument? This argument-based approach often leads to an "aha" moment for those I teach it to (as it did for me), and it's my mission to spread it further. I hope it helps you.

Now, as you craft your argument, you'll make claims and support those claims with proof. Remember, your claims need solid support. The great copywriter Gary Bencivenga once said, "I have always advised my clients to build their products squarely on their strongest proof elements."[2]

A lack of proof in marketing—after not thinking through a customer's beliefs—is the second biggest mistake I see smart people make in their business.

Both mistakes can be avoided by answering the question: What does my customer need to believe in order to buy? Then, once you identify those beliefs, you argue for them. You tell your reader, "Here is my argument for why you should believe X and then Y and now Z."

Let's dive deeper and see just how claims and proof work.

---

1   Joanna Garner and Michael Alley, "How the Design of Presentation Slides Affects Audience Comprehension: A Case for the Assertion-Evidence Approach," International Journal of Engineering Education, 29, (2013: 1564-1579).
2   Gary Bencivenga, "The Secret of How to Sell Anything," Gary Bencivenga's Marketing Bullets, (Bullet 29) https://marketingbullets.com/bullet-29/.

The Claim/Proof Model

I developed this claim/proof model as a simple (but powerful) way to help business owners create persuasive communication. You can use this model in any area of your life to win people over to your way of thinking.

Claim/proof is everywhere. It's the source code of persuasive human communication. In the remainder of this chapter and the next, I'll detail its universality. Later, Tiago will show you how to create marketing content using the claim/proof model.

Claim/Proof in Brand Advertising

Let's start with an example that is close to our marketing discussion. Then we'll study two more outside-the-box examples.

Consider the brand advertisements you often see on TV during major events like the Super Bowl. These ads, although heavy on visuals and light on text, still adhere to the claim/proof model.

Imagine a commercial from a car company showcasing their latest outdoor vehicle. In one scene, the vehicle climbs a rugged mountain. In the next scene, it forges through a river, water dramatically splashing around it.

What's the underlying claim that this car advertisement is making? That this car is tough.

Notice how the claim isn't explicitly stated but is implied through the actions depicted. The visuals of the car tackling extreme terrain serve as proof supporting the claim.

Here's a summary of the ad in terms of claim/proof:
Claim: This car is tough.
Proof: The commercial shows the car driving in extreme environments.

See how that works? Here's another example.

Claim/Proof in Stand-Up Comedy

Many stand-up comedy routines thrive on the claim/proof structure. Here's how: The comedian begins with a claim—a statement of truth that amuses the audience with its relatability.

As anticipation builds, the comedian delivers the proof, and the audience erupts in laughter, recognizing the truth in the humorous evidence provided.

Some comedians might offer just one example of proof before moving on, while others can spend up to twenty minutes elaborating on a single claim.

Consider a familiar category of humor that elicits both groans and laughter: dad jokes.

Imagine a dad who fancies himself a budding stand-up comedian. As he drives his kids to school, he sees an opportunity for his routine.

"My kids are obsessed with technology," he says with a smirk.

The kids groan, sensing what's coming.

Dad delivers. "When I suggest they watch a sunrise, they Google it."

And he doesn't stop there . . .

"When I serve vegetables, they swipe left."

"Their idea of a power nap? Recharging their smartphones."

While these may make you cringe, they perfectly illustrate the claim/proof format.

Claim: My kids are obsessed with technology.
Proof: Simple yet relatable examples that illustrate (and exaggerate) the kids' tech dependency.

Chris Rock, a master of stand-up who uses this structure, discusses it in the TV special, *Talking Funny*. He points out that newer comedians often mistake the setup (the claim) for the punchline (the proof).[3]

For example, saying "My kids are obsessed with technology" isn't the punchline—it's the setup. The actual humor comes from the proof—the examples that underline the kids' tech obsession.

Rock emphasizes that failing to provide proof leaves the audience unsatisfied.

Does that sound familiar? It's the same critique we make of much marketing material. Just as comedians must support their claims to deliver a successful joke, marketers must support their claims to win over customers.

---

3   Jerry Seinfeld, Chris Rock, Ricky Gervais, and Louis C.K., Talking Funny, directed by John Moffitt, (New York, NY: HBO Studio Productions), aired April 20, 2011 on HBO. https://www.youtube.com/watch?v=OKY6BGcx37k.

Whether in comedy or marketing, the power lies in proving your point.

Claim/Proof in Movies

Let's look at movies. In this final example, you'll see the true universality of claim/proof and how it's woven into so much of communication, media, and entertainment.

I have a young daughter, so a movie that's constantly playing on our TV is Disney's *Moana*. (I also never met an adult who didn't enjoy *Moana*—it's awesome.)[4]

No, *Moana* isn't selling a product. Yet, it's still selling us a belief, getting us to buy into the movie's story.

Choosing the core message in stories, like in Disney's *Moana*, is a big deal. In Disney movies, one message is eternal: the hero is always brave. To prove this claim, Disney shows the hero performing courageous acts. The story, characters, and scenes are carefully orchestrated to prove Moana's bravery.

Look at how Moana departs her island to go on an adventure. Nobody in her village had done that before. So, seeing Moana leave her home makes us think, "Wow, that girl sure is brave."

Claim: Moana is brave.
Proof: She sails away from her island.

The *way* Moana leaves home also matters. Does she leave on a big, safe yacht? No way. She builds a small, shaky raft and sails over giant waves.

Claim: Moana is brave.
Proof: She sails in a shaky raft over giant waves.

The music plays a part, too. It's intense and ominous, making the scene feel more dangerous. How can you dramatize *your* proof points?

Claim: Moana is brave.
Proof: Intense, scary music plays during her journey.

---

4   Ron Clements, John Musker, Don Hall, and Chris Williams, directors, Moana, (2016; Burbank, CA: Walt Disney Animation Studios), streaming through Disney+.

Notice how the proof points can be a multi-sensory experience?

Each of these examples is a way Disney backs up the claim that Moana is brave.

How to Weave Proof into Your Marketing

First, nail down *what* you want to say—your claim. Then, decide *how* you'll say it—your proof.

Connect your claims to the beliefs required for your customer to buy. Flood your content with proof. Throw in colors, sounds, feelings— the whole shebang. Hit your point from every angle. Make your case bulletproof.

You can see how marketing is a choreography between assertion and creativity. Claims are straightforward statements that convey the value or promise of a product or service—proving those claims brings in much creativity.

Looking at marketing through this new lens, do you see how it can be fun? Imagine that.

In the next chapter, we'll go deeper into the proof element and give you several different types of proof you can use to back up your marketing claims.

CHAPTER NINE

Build Belief Part 2

By BILLY BROAS

Making claims is critical to marketing. It's how we guide your prospects down the right path for them.

When we fail to make claims, our marketing becomes diluted, leaving our prospects unsure of our conviction and expertise. Our prospects move on to competitors who state their stances boldly.

The following is an example of a business owner who took a stand in her marketing content. Given that these two chapters on claim/proof are best understood using the legal example, let's stick with that theme.

At a recent lunch, I met an estate planning attorney, Aisha Williams. Tough story—her family was torn apart when her grandfather passed away and his affairs were a jumbled mess. He had a simple will containing many holes that resulted in major conflict among his children. Some of his children still do not speak to this day.

She's now on a mission to save families from the same fate. She does so by educating families on what they must have in place when that tragic day arrives and a loved one passes away.

In her business, she makes the claim, "A will alone is not enough."

She stands firmly behind this claim. And why wouldn't she? She believes in what she's saying, and she has the experience to prove her claim.

This is the leadership your prospects want. They want service providers, business owners, and companies who take a stand. They want an expert to stand up and say, "Here's what I've seen, and here's what I recommend."

When it comes to your area of expertise, you have a preferred way of doing things. Every smart person I've met does. It's time to stand behind your methodology and argue for it publicly. To do so will involve making claims.

But as we covered, you also need *proof*.

When you speak on your recommended approach, don't just say, "Here's what I recommend." Instead, say, "Here's what I recommend, and *here's why*."

That second part—the "here's why"—is where proof enters the equation.

Sure, it would be nice if our claims alone got the job done. It would be nice if our estate planning attorney could simply tell her prospects a will alone is not enough, and they'd listen to her and immediately create an estate plan.

But claims alone don't do the job; we need to prove our claims. And frankly, isn't that the way it should be? Backing up claims is how we stay honest. Imagine if every marketer supported their claims with proof? The world might be a better place.

The next section will show you how to use proof to back up your claims. But first, let's clear up a couple of misconceptions about that word—*proof*.

The First Misconception about Proof

When I say the word *proof* in a marketing context, I am commonly met with, "Billy is talking about proof that the product works."

That reaction makes sense. You can imagine an inventor revealing their new gizmo and proclaiming, "I've finally made it work!" and the inventor's friend responding, "Oh yeah? Prove it."

In that simplistic scenario, yes, *proof* refers to proof the product works. But we live in the real world, and the real world is more nuanced. We're marketing products that are often hard to understand, and we're trying to reach people who might not yet even recognize their problem.

So, the whole "proof means proof the product works" concept is too simplistic. Proof *includes* proof that the product works. But you need far more proof points than that.

Additionally, when we talk about proof that a product works, what do we even mean by "work"?

The word "work" implies some sort of standard or measurement of success. And it's unlikely that 100% of the customers of a particular product would agree on that measurement.

I enjoy our living room couch because it's comfortable, but my wife enjoys it because it looks nice. She and I have different measurements of product success when it comes to our couch.

So, be careful when you hear someone say the product works. What do they mean? Truth is, that phrase is an oversimplification of the real-world buying and consuming experience.

Besides, most of your prospect's objections aren't around the effectiveness of your product. Most objections arise long before a person is considering swiping their credit card.

For example, an "objection" to the estate planning attorney's services may not be about her fees or if you'll meet with her in person or over Zoom. One of her prospects' objections could be they don't even realize they have a problem.

They might be saying instead, "I don't need an estate plan."

That doesn't sound like what we normally think of as an objection. We think of an objection as something like, "Whoa, whoa, whoa . . . that's way too much money."

But price objections only come into play if you reach a discussion about price, and unfortunately, most prospects never get that far.

Let's think about the early objection an estate attorney must overcome. Let's imagine that in this attorney's town lives a retired man who drafted a will but not an estate plan. Should the attorney provide him with proof that they're good at their job? That they work fast and their fees are reasonable?

Those proof points don't make much sense at this stage in the communication. After all, the retired man hasn't even considered an estate plan, let alone shopped for an attorney.

How does our attorney reach this man and, if it's a good fit for both, offer him their services?

Our attorney must make claims. The retired man doesn't know anything about estate planning. He has a long chain of beliefs ahead of him, and the only way for our attorney to take him down that chain to the point where he creates an estate plan is to make claims.

But proof must follow every claim, right? So, we must provide proof, although it's clearly not the previously mentioned type of proof. It's not proof of the effectiveness of the lawyer's services—the retired man hasn't gotten that far yet.

You now see why proof doesn't only come into play when talking about your product or service. Proof comes into play much earlier in the buying process.

The Second Misconception about Proof

Proof does not always mean scientific proof. In this day and age, we're very scientifically minded. We hear the word "proof" and we instantly think of lab results, data charts, and empirical studies.

But think about our end goal—we're communicating with a person. Do you require scientific proof for every decision you make throughout your day? No way.

You make decisions all the time without scientific proof, and very often, you're happy with those decisions. Even if you saw concrete lab results that proved a product's effectiveness, you're more likely to follow the recommendation of a trusted friend.

Imagine you were looking for a new laundromat. You might read an article stating that a local laundromat won an award in your city for being #1 at removing stains. It was scientifically proven by an outside organization.

"They sound perfect," you think. Then you bring it up with your brother and he tells you, "No, don't go to that laundromat. They're awful."

You decide to go somewhere else. So much for scientific proof.

For my attorney friend, in order to address her prospect's early objections, what type of proof might she use?

Remember the claim she must make? "A will is not enough."

The proof needs to back up that particular claim. In this case, her proof point might be a story. In fact, her own story of her family's tragic ordeal with their grandfather would be an excellent proof point to back up her claim.

Her prospect, the retired man, might hear her story and think to himself, "Wow, I guess a will alone is not enough. I better get an estate plan."

Because of the attorney's story, the man now has the belief, "A will alone is not enough."

Our proof point worked. We could use other forms of proof, too.

If we want to go the more scientific route, that's no problem. Scientific forms of proof are an effective arrow in our quiver.

Our attorney's scientific proof point might be something like, "I analyzed the estate of everyone who passed away in California who had a will but no estate plan, and over the past fifty years, it's taken double the time on average to release an estate to its heirs."

Pretty good proof point.

So we have a personal story, we have data . . . What else might we use to prove our claim that a will is not enough?

How about an analogy?

Our attorney might publish an informational brochure that begins, "Having only a will is like locking your front door but leaving the windows wide open; you've taken a step for security, but your assets are still vulnerable to probate delays and disputes."

You can imagine the retired man picking up this brochure, reading this analogy, and thinking, "That makes sense. Maybe a will alone is not enough. Let me keep reading . . ."

Again, our proof point did its job.

Using our estate attorney example, let's summarize the two misconceptions about proof. First, our attorney made a claim and provided proof that had nothing to do with the effectiveness of her legal services. Instead, her claim targeted beliefs far earlier in her prospect's chain of beliefs. Her claim was, "A will alone is not enough."

If her claim is not believed by the prospect, any claim about the effectiveness of her legal services is irrelevant. The prospect will never get that far.

Second, she backed up her claim using various forms of proof—not just scientific proof. We brainstormed three different types of proof:

1. A personal story.
2. A scientific study.
3. An analogy.

Do you see how there's much nuance to *proof*?

Now, our attorney might run with one of those proof points, or she may use all three. She may even tailor her proof point to the particular person. If she's speaking to an engineer, she may use the research study. If she's speaking to an artist, she may use the visual analogy.

Part of marketing is understanding your customer and learning what types of messaging and proof points resonate best with them.

To be safe, we recommend you sprinkle in a variety of proof types. It will make your argument more robust, interesting, and compelling. And if you learn that a certain type of proof resonates more with your audience, awesome. Double down on it.

Proof does the job of getting the prospect to accept our claim—that's it.

Treat people as humans, not robots. Mix up your forms of proof. Weave in emotion with one proof point, and then share a data chart in the next. Make it engaging and interesting for your prospect.

By making claims and backing them up with various forms of proof, you'll be educating your prospects. It will feel good, too. You've got nothing to hide. You're laying out the issues and making the case for your recommended solution. And if they want you to help them implement that solution—great.

Proof is how you get your point across. Now that you know how to use a variety of types of proof, you might want a more comprehensive list of proof types. We've got you covered.

For this, we return to our old friends, the ancient Greeks.

Argue like Aristotle

Aristotle developed three concepts to help influence an audience: ethos, pathos, and logos.

Ethos: To remember the definition of ethos, first think of the word "ethic." It sounds similar. Then ask, "Am I an ethical person?" (I hope that answer is yes, by the way.)

That little trick is how I remember the definition of ethos, because ethos refers to the character of the person making the argument. Ethos establishes trust. It reassures your reader that you (or your sources) are reliable and authoritative.

Ethos can show up through various avenues, including:

- Expert opinions or authoritative figures in the field.
- Testimonials from individuals who have benefited from your product.
- Data taken from research studies that support your claim.
- Third-party reviews that lend an external voice of approval.

Ethos lends weight to your words, making them resonate more profoundly.

Pathos: Pathos is an appeal to emotion. For the word pathos, you can think of "pathology," which is the study of disease. Disease, of course, leads to suffering and negative emotions.

Not too cheery, I know, but it's simply a way to remember the definition. But pathos doesn't need to be negative. It can—and should—also invoke positive emotions.

So when you're using pathos, you appeal to emotions—positive and negative.

In decision-making, emotions play an undeniable role. Again, humans aren't robots. A common misconception, often among analytical minds, is to undervalue emotional appeal in communication, dismissing it as unnecessary or even inappropriate.

Being dismissive of pathos is a common mistake people make, and it's especially common among smart people. Analytical minds often look at emotion with skepticism, even resentment.

Our human emotions are not something to resent. They're a beautiful part of being human. If you've ever been excited about achieving a goal, your excitement was an emotion. And it's unlikely you'd be as motivated to pursue that goal without the emotion of excitement. So emotions play an important role in our journey toward achieving goals.

Emotion, when woven into your marketing content, becomes a powerful way to connect with your prospect and get your point across.

Using pathos in your proof points might mean:

- Sharing stories that evoke empathy, joy, or other emotions.
- Using imagery that symbolizes deeper sentiments or values.
- Writing words that are vivid and stoke the desires of your prospect.

When you use pathos, you show the other person you respect them by treating them like a human, not a robot.

You also respect your prospects in the sense that you know they are intelligent. You know your prospects can think for themselves and make well-reasoned decisions. And that's where our next type of proof enters the equation.

Logos: This proof point is easiest to remember because it resembles the word "logic."

You know you've used logic effectively when a prospect reads your marketing content, nods their head, and says, "That makes sense."

When they do this, your prospect is recognizing the logical structure of your argument, even if they don't express it in such formal terms—like Spock from *Star Trek* would, saying, "That is the logical choice, Captain."

When using logos, consider the following strategies:

- Explain the mechanics of how your product or service works.
- Map out a clear and coherent path that shows your prospect how you get them from *problem* to *problem solved*.
- Give a clear demonstration of how the value of your product exceeds its cost.

Logos can be especially useful if you need to win over a team of people, as in B2B selling, for example, where one person's emotions are less likely to factor into the group decision compared to, say, selling to an individual.

(At the same time, even in B2B settings, the decision to write the check often comes down to one person, and it would be wise to consider that person's emotions.)

Ethos, pathos, and logos do not operate in isolation. Each plays a role in a blended marketing message that becomes memorable, persuasive, and empowering.

Let's recap our Belief Building process:

Step 1: Pick the Belief. Find the main idea or belief you want to share with your audience.

Step 2: Make a Claim. Turn that belief into a simple statement or message.

Step 3: Prove It. Show that your message is true. Use stories, facts, or examples to make it real and believable.

Now that you know the formula, I'll turn it over to Tiago for an example of how he implements all three elements in the marketing for his online course.

CHAPTER TEN

Let's Create Some Marketing Content

By TIAGO FORTE

Billy just showed you the process for Belief Building. Now let's put it into action. We'll take a shot at creating some marketing content using the Belief Building approach.

First, our process:

Step One: Nail down what we want to say. This is our claim. The claim should instill a predetermined belief, which is required for purchasing our product.

Step Two: Support our claim with proof. We can use ethos, pathos, and logos to mix and match our proof elements.

Step Three: Create our content. Flood our content with claims, proof, sights, sounds, and feelings. We'll make a compelling case for our recommended way of doing things.*

Ready?

Let's pretend we are creating content that will eventually lead to the sale of my online course on productivity, *Building a Second Brain*.

Example 1: LinkedIn Post

We'll begin with a LinkedIn post. As a marketing channel, LinkedIn is a platform for professionals, so if you're doing B2B or if you want to target your customers by profession, it's a great option.

In this LinkedIn post, we'll attempt to instill the belief: I am being held back by information overwhelm.

Why this belief? Because if someone doesn't believe information overwhelm is a problem, how likely are they to buy a course that solves it?

Now, in my experience, the reader I'm targeting already has some sense that information overwhelm is a problem in their life. But it might not be top of mind.

You must remember that you are not your prospect. Your topic is top of mind all day for you because it's your business. But it's not theirs, and your prospects have a thousand other problems they're dealing with.

That means we can't take this belief—"Information overwhelm is holding me back"—for granted. We need to speak to the problem. That way, our reader will be open to a discussion on how to fix it.

The first step is to identify our inputs for our LinkedIn post. Let's use the info below.

Belief: Information overwhelm is holding me back.
Claim: Information overwhelm is bad and only getting worse.
Proof: Data from a Nielsen study. (logos)
Format: Text + Image.
Marketing Channel: LinkedIn.
Call-to-action: Leave a comment.

*You can get templates for this chapter by scanning the QR code at the front of the book or by going to simplemarketingbook.com/bonus

Now, the output.

The LinkedIn Post

Can you believe this number?

A 2020 report from Nielsen shows that Americans now spend over twelve hours each day consuming media. And that was before the pandemic, before people became even more attached to their smartphones.[1]

Just imagine it—half of our time, which means half of our lives, is spent interacting with the digital world.

We are trying to run complex modern lives on a brain that hasn't fundamentally changed in 200,000 years. We are trying to run twenty-first-century lives on Paleolithic hardware.

Think about the content you've consumed over, say, the past month: the books and articles you've read, the podcasts you've listened to, the YouTube videos you've watched, and the conversations you've had.

When you consider how much time you've invested . . . what do you have to show for all that?

Can you say what you learned from the last book you read or YouTube video you watched? Can you point to one useful takeaway from the last course you took?

If not, how do you know you learned anything at all?

I want you to be very honest with yourself: What is the return on investment of the up to twelve hours per day you spend consuming content? What concrete value have you taken away from that staggering amount of time?

The very first step in making any change is realizing you have a problem. And that is the only step I'll ask you to take today: acknowledge that your relationship to information isn't working.

It's not working. It's not okay. It's not necessary or acceptable.

Leave a comment below and tell me how you deal with information overload.

---

1   To visually show you this, check out the chart of the Nielsen study. That would strengthen the proof. Pallavibhoj and Pallavibhoj, "The Nielsen Total Audience Report Hub," Nielsen, November 2, 2023, https://www.nielsen.com/insights/2021/total-audience-advertising-across-todays-media/.

You don't need to be a professional copywriter to write this. And the thinking behind the post does 90% of the heavy lifting. Once we identify our inputs, the output (i.e. the writing) is much easier.

Do you think you could create content more consistently if you followed this formula?

Example 2: Email

Next up, we'll write an email. In addition to using a different marketing channel, we'll use a different belief and form of proof.

The belief we'll target for this one will be: A Second Brain can benefit my career.

My reader needs this belief. As opposed to the first example, which targeted a belief related to the problem, this belief focuses on the *solution*. I need to show people that a "Second Brain" (my trademark term for a personal note-taking system) can fit seamlessly into their lives and provide tangible benefits to their careers.

For this email's proof, I'm going to tell a story. It could be anyone's story, but I'll use a personal one. This is something that really happened to me, and it does a very convincing job of showing the benefit of having a Second Brain. As you're reading the email, read it on two tracks. First, read the email just like a normal subscriber would. At the same time, read it as a student of Belief Building. Do you see how my proof backs up my claim and why that claim is needed in the first place?

Here we go:

Belief: A Second Brain can benefit my career.
Claim: When you have a tight deadline, a Second Brain can save you.
Proof: Tiago's personal story. (pathos)
Format: Text.
Marketing Channel: Email.
Call-to-action: Enroll in the online course.

The Email

Subject: My Dream Project Arrived at the Worst Possible Time

After months of intense effort, I was getting ready to launch the first version of my online course. We were only days away from the kick-off and I was at the end of my physical and psychological limits.

That's when the email hit my inbox: Toyota wanted to hire me to deliver a full-day workshop to a group of fourteen executives.

I could hardly believe it. One of the world's most influential companies, originator of many of the principles that informed my work, wanted my help.

This email was the opportunity of a lifetime.

But there was a catch. The workshop took place in three days. Another speaker had fallen through, and they needed someone to step in on short notice.

I took in a deep breath, collapsed back in my chair, and stared at the ceiling in disbelief. How could I do it? How would it be possible?

Normally, I would spend at least a full week preparing for a project like this one. I would review tons of ideas, research dozens of different options, and coordinate closely with the client over several in-depth phone calls.

None of that was possible. With a mere two days to prepare, I didn't have time for so much as an hour of new research. I only had time to use the knowledge and resources I already had at my disposal.

Such moments are pivotal turning points in our businesses, our careers, and our lives. The best opportunities arrive when you least expect them, and often when you have many other things going on.

At such a moment, you are faced with a choice. You can step beyond your usual way of doing things and discover a new path or even identity. Or you don't, and always wonder what could have been.

Fortunately, I had an advantage. It's a secret weapon that gives me far more options in the face of any challenge: my Second Brain.

It's a personal system for preserving my most valuable knowledge for the moments I need it most.

For the Toyota workshop, I set a timer for thirty minutes and began searching my Second Brain for any relevant content I'd kept over the years. To my amazement, I found I already possessed a wealth of knowledge about the topic I would be facilitating.

Despite not knowing I would ever face such an opportunity, I had already collected tons of rich material: examples, research, case studies, diagrams, explanations, and even slides I'd created in the past.

It was as if I had spent months and years preparing for a moment I didn't even know was coming. And because of all that unconscious preparation, I was able to say yes to Toyota. And as I delivered my workshop, with all this supporting material at hand, I felt completely confident as a twenty-something standing up there in front of those senior executives.

A Second Brain can be your secret weapon, too. You don't have to be limited to drawing only on your best ideas at one moment; you can store and access the best ideas of your life, adding your ideas to the work of hundreds of the world's smartest thinkers throughout history.

When the next opportunity comes along, will you be prepared?

If you want to be ready, start building your Second Brain today. Click here to learn more about our online course that helps you build one, step-by-step.

See you on the inside,

Tiago

Notice how the story leads you to this conclusion: a Second Brain can benefit you in your career.

We identified that required belief long before we sat down to write the email. Do you see how doing this work upfront can save you time later? It makes a big difference.

Okay, one more example. This time, we'll create a visual content piece.

Example 3: Instagram Post

Instagram is a visuals-first platform, so if visuals resonate more with your customers, Instagram could be a good marketing channel to test.

The belief we'll target for this Instagram post is, "A notebook is a secret weapon of top creatives."

Many artists, photographers, branding experts, and other creatives enroll in our course, so this post should appeal to them.

For the form of proof, we'll use ethos in order to appeal to someone's character and credibility. There are many ways I could use ethos for a post, but we'll give a historical example. We'll use Leonardo da Vinci, who was famous for his notebook and is well respected by creatives for his multiple talents.

Let's create a Leonardo da Vinci Instagram post!

First, our inputs:

Belief: A notebook is a secret weapon of top creatives.

Claim: Top thinkers and creatives relied on notebooks throughout history.

Proof: Leonardo da Vinci. (ethos)

Format: Text + Image.

Marketing Channel: Instagram.

Call-to-action: Enter your email address for a free PDF.

Image:

Image notes: The main image should be a picture from Leonardo da Vinci's notebook. The image below was taken from the public domain. Make sure you follow the copyright rules for any third party images you post online.

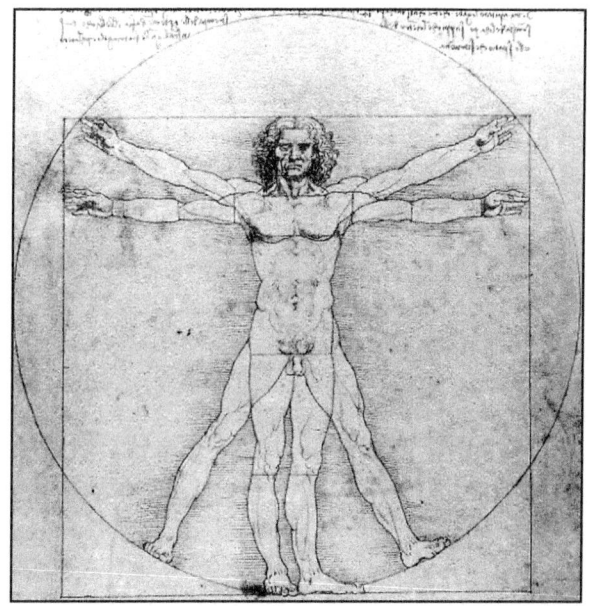

Instagram Caption:
Did you know Leonardo da Vinci, the epitome of Renaissance brilliance, had a secret weapon? It was his notebooks. Historians have uncovered over 13,000 pages of his drawings, ideas, and inventions.

What if you applied da Vinci's notebook habit to the digital era? What might you be able to remember? What might you be able to create?

Click the link in my bio to get a free PDF where I break down each of da Vinci's note-taking techniques and how they can be applied in the digital realm. It will help you get started building your very own *digital* notebook to preserve and cultivate your best ideas.

After writing my Instagram post, I might employ two or three tactics to help it get the most visibility, like:

- Add popular hashtags.
- Turn the post into an Instagram reel.
- Encourage readers to leave a comment to win a prize.

These tactics would pour fuel on my fire and gain additional reach for my persuasive messaging.[2]

It Can Be This Simple

Do you see how those three posts each create a compelling case for buying my course? I hit on a variety of beliefs, used a variety of mediums, and changed up the call to action.

I've found that not only does approaching your content from this angle make it easier to create that content, but it will attract better customers, too.

There are three ways you can gain customers:

1. Drag someone in, kicking and screaming, using heavy-handed persuasion tactics and manipulation.
2. Crank out endless random content, hoping that because you've been so generous, people will buy.

---

2   Leonardo da Vinci's Vitruvian Man illustration are all over the internet. I found this one at https://en.wikipedia.org/wiki/Vitruvian_Man#/media/File:Da_Vinci_Vitruve_Luc_Viatour.jpg.

3. Our approach: give your customer agency by making a strong case for your recommended path, and then let the prospect make the best decision for them.

Free content is a much-discussed issue in online marketing, so let's explore it deeper.

How Do You Approach Free Content?

After years of creating free content, I've learned what needs to go in the content versus what needs to be left out. Most online entrepreneurs haven't learned this lesson yet.

Many smart people are publishing content online, but they're publishing what I call "implementation details."

What are implementation details?

If my team is having a meeting and suddenly someone begins talking about the ConvertKit (our email software) template they think we should use for an upcoming product launch, I'll say, "Those are just implementation details."

Or another employee might ask, "Should I make the website in Wix or WordPress?"

"Those are implementation details," I respond.

It's my way of saying, "That decision is downstream. Right now, we need to be focused upstream on the more needle-moving decisions."

Similarly, in your marketing, don't burden your prospects with implementation details. Customers first need the education to even find the classroom. They need the preliminary information to even understand what is being talked about. They need to know if they're even on the right path.

What I call implementation details, Billy calls "hard teaching," and it was one of the earliest and most eye-opening shifts for me.

Nobody likes hard selling—being repeatedly and relentlessly told to buy without having your questions and concerns addressed. It's disrespectful and offensive.

But one of the biggest mistakes I see online business owners make is hard teaching—overwhelming their followers with so much "value" they don't have time to even consider the product on offer.

Online creators generate an endless supply of tutorials, ultimate guides, walk-throughs, PDF reports, and live workshops, stuffing more and more information down their potential customers' throats.

They give away all their best content, hoping and praying that if they just give out enough free stuff, people will somehow magically buy their product.

But what people actually need is . . . your product!

They need the structure and the accountability and yes, the skin-in-the-game of truly committing—not yet another 5,000-word blog post.

When you keep giving them implementation details instead of meeting them at their current beliefs and taking them to the next step—which should eventually lead to a product offering—you actually delay the sale.

Worse, you attract freebie-seekers and tire-kickers. Why would they buy the paid product or service if they can't even keep up with all the free stuff you're throwing at them?

Free content can be great if you approach it correctly. Rather than stacking encyclopedias upon people's outstretched arms, free content should educate prospects to make the best decision for them. In other words, our free content approach helps them become more empowered buyers.

This happens naturally when you follow the Belief Building approach we outlined.

As you begin engaging people with your content, prospects start asking questions they think are the right ones. But to be an effective teacher, you need to push back. Remember, you have to get your prospects to ask the right questions.

When you create content based around Belief Building, you are many times challenging their basic assumptions. And when you hit on a missing or incorrect belief, you'll know it. It's like hitting a nerve, and will send an unmistakable electric jolt through your followers that will show up as comments, messages, and yes, sales.

Testing Beliefs with Your Marketing Content

I grew my business in the early days mostly via Twitter (now X) as my main marketing channel. I saw every tweet as a ping, a little test.

What do people think about this?

What are the existing beliefs around this?

What is the conversation that's happening around this belief?

Often, a tweet I thought would go viral would instead yield crickets. That told me people didn't care about that particular belief. It didn't strike a nerve.

And then a tweet I thought was going to go nowhere, goes viral. You can do the same thing on LinkedIn, in your email newsletter, or whatever channel you choose.

Every day, you get to test a new belief. Imagine if every email and piece of content you're putting out gave you an opportunity to test a belief. How often would you do that? As often as you possibly could, right? Because you're accelerating your learning.

You can see how the Belief Building approach to free content is different from most. It's intentional content. It has direction instead of being random. And best of all, this approach to content creates a win-win for both you and your prospect.

It's not about chasing the next shiny object. It's about sticking to the basics. It's about studying your buyer's psychology like an anthropologist, and creating a system for speaking to it. Nobody can do that for you. It represents the critical keystone in all your marketing efforts.

Marketing with Integrity

If you think about it, communication is everything.

If you look at your life, your life happens through communication. The way you speak to your family and your loved ones, the way you listen (or don't listen) to them. The way you communicate with your peers, your colleagues, your boss, and yes, your customers. It's all communication. That's human life. We are social beings.

You are probably a decent communicator in real life. But then, suddenly, you go on the internet and you're a different person.

You're not standing in front of someone talking with them. You have to learn a completely different kind of communication for online spaces.

You have to learn how to communicate through email, how to communicate on social media, and with hundreds or thousands of people you'll likely never meet.

When I started seriously studying my followers' psychology, my marketing was earning a failing grade. I was constantly telling my subscribers the "what" but not the "why."

"Hi there, I created a new module."

But why should someone care? Why should they click the blue link in the email?

I learned I had to sell *every click*, even if he or she was already a customer. You may be tempted to think, "Oh, they're already in the course. They're committed."

But no. Even with your existing customers, you must sell every click. If you don't, they won't click it. And eventually, they'll forget about you.

For the vast majority of products and services I see being sold online, these questions are in dire need of answers:

- Why should your customers care?
- How are you different?
- Why should they trust you?

You can have every other aspect of your product perfectly designed, but if you don't take the time to understand your customer and how you can help them, no one will ever experience what you have to offer.

The marketing I'm talking about isn't mere "promotion." It's not just talking indiscriminately about your product to anyone who will listen.

I'm talking about marketing as product development. Marketing as user research. Marketing as content creation. Marketing as world-building. Marketing as customer service. Marketing as deep empathy.

I'm talking about marketing that is so good, selling becomes unnecessary because people sell *themselves* on it. Your marketing message is the core, the linchpin of your products.

Once I got over the hump and started to see my new marketing efforts paying off, I breathed a sigh of relief. All those things I thought I had to do in marketing might help, but they weren't necessary.

Here's what I decided I *won't do* in marketing:

- No unethical, high-pressure sales tactics.
- No complex funnels with endless sub-branches.
- No obnoxious countdown timers with fake urgency.
- No artificial social proof with "anonymous" testimonials.
- No "limited time" offers that aren't actually limited.
- No relentless self-promotion on social media.
- No "live" webinars you can watch any hour of the day.

You read that right. You can skip probably 90% of what most people think of when they hear "online marketing."

Here's what I *do* practice in marketing:

- Clear and persuasive copywriting.
- Classic, heartfelt storytelling that speaks to people's everyday problems.
- A strong and well-communicated differentiator, so I stand out from the competition.
- An email list I control and regularly provide value to.
- Informative, insightful content that delivers value upfront while also moving people toward a sale.
- Long-term relationships that will continue to bear fruit for years.
- Authentic testimonials that help people see themselves in what I'm offering.

In other words, it is possible to trust and respect your customers while earning their trust and respect in return. It is possible to have people look forward to your promotions because they provide so much value.

Growing up with an artist as a father, there was never any question that what he was creating was art, and that it deserved every bit of attention and money people lavished on it. I've taken that same attitude into my work as an online creator and entrepreneur, and I suggest you do the same.

You are pouring your heart and soul into your work. You care deeply about people and are dedicated to serving them in the best way you know how. Your purpose and values are intertwined with every decision you make and action you take, and the ideas you're putting out into the world are therefore the truest expressions of who you are.

And who you are deserves a bigger stage. I sincerely hope you take the principles in this book and use them to find that stage.

CHAPTER ELEVEN

Spot the Pattern

By BILLY BROAS

Look at anything being sold and you'll see Belief Building. Once you see its pattern, you can't unsee it. And then you can use it to create better products and stronger marketing.

What if I told you that even your grocery store's aisles are packed with ideas on how to improve your marketing? Here, we'll play a game to demonstrate.

Below, I'm going to list some everyday household items. Read through them, and as you're doing so, imagine yourself purchasing these items.

Ready? Here we go:

- Milk
- Dish soap
- Socks
- Laundry detergent
- Sponges
- Shampoo
- Bath towels
- Trash bags
- Lightbulbs
- Eight-week executive coaching program for CEOs

Did that last one catch you off-guard? Not exactly a household item, is it? Did you feel the resistance when you hit the coaching program?

That resistance was you bumping into the world of Belief Building.

You probably have an intuition that the coaching program is fundamentally different from the grocery store products, but what's the *actual* difference?

Is it because the everyday items are physical products and the coaching program is a service? Is it the difference in cost? The complexity of the product?

It's all those things. But also try looking at this list through the lens of what you've just learned in this book. There is another big factor that separates the coaching program from the grocery store items: Belief Building.

To show you the pattern, let's return to the grocery store. We'll pick an item and show you how its backstory is a microcosm of how all products get marketed and sold.

Selling Fancy Eggs

Let's walk inside the grocery store and head to the egg aisle. As we peer into the chilly refrigerator, what do we see?

A plain, gray, cardboard egg carton. Commodity chicken eggs. Nothing fancy.

These commodity eggs are easy-to-understand products. People "get it," and that's why you don't see the egg companies dedicating much copywriting to their marketing. Have you ever read a long sales page to buy a $1.99 carton of eggs? Of course not.

Why is that? Because the egg companies don't need to do much Belief Building for you to buy commodity eggs. It's more a question of how much they cost.

—People buy eggs on price and go for the cheapest. At least that was the case before fancy eggs hit the shelves.

I remember it well . . .

First, organic eggs arrived. Then free-range eggs. Then pasture-raised, grass-fed, omega-fortified, and on and on.

When these fancy eggs hit the market, eggs suddenly became more complicated. That's when you saw the egg companies turning to our favorite marketing approach: Belief Building.

You see, when marketing a commodity product, you have one primary way to compete: price.

In Belief Building terms, when it comes to products like commodity eggs, customers are *fully aware*. That's a copywriting term for customers who have no (or a very small) gap between their current beliefs and the beliefs needed in order to purchase the product.

Compare cheap chicken eggs to the fancy egg examples we've shared in this book, like my beer brewing course or Tiago's productivity course. In those cases, our audience didn't know what they didn't know, which meant we had to educate them.

The egg market is an interesting because, for decades, you had a product that was viewed as a commodity. Then, with the introduction of these fancy eggs, a new marketing need arose, and we saw Belief Building in action.

Do you remember when the fancy eggs first hit the market? Ever see their cartons with little booklets attached?

The job of those booklets was to explain this new product to customers by answering questions like, "What does organic mean? Why is organic better for you?"

And so on.

Egg companies had to provide those educational booklets to make the case for why a customer should shell out (couldn't help it) $5 instead of the usual $1.50 per dozen. Egg companies decided to *de-commoditize* their products and raise prices, which in turn required Belief Building.

Even though it's been years since fancy eggs hit the market and customers are now more aware, you still see this Belief Building process in action.

Here's a screenshot from the website of an egg company we have in San Diego, called Happy Egg Company.

Happy Egg Free Range

Our hens have 8+ hours a day of outdoor access to forage and play, with shade trees and play kits for shelter. They spend the night in the barn for protection from predators.

Examine that image. Look for our claim/proof model. What do you see?

Right out of the gate, in the top banner, you see one major claim. It's woven into the company's name: these chickens are happy.

Just like Disney determined that Moana being brave was important to their audience, Happy Egg Company, through their market research, determined that happy chickens were important to their customers.[1]

Then, in the large graphic below the banner, you see ample proof for that claim. Using our Greek forms of proof, we see:

- **Logos:** Data in the form of the hours spent outside and the acreage the chickens have free to roam.
- **Pathos:** The storytelling: "Our chickens play all day and spend the night protected from predators."

---

1   If you want to see the full website for the Happy Egg Company, you can find them here: https://happyegg.com/.

- **Ethos:** Being free range and USDA-certified organic, the company leverages the credibility of a government agency.

Pretty neat, huh? Aristotle would be proud of this website.

Are You Selling Commodity Eggs or Fancy Eggs?

The better a customer understands a product, the less copy is needed to educate them. The worse a customer understands a product, the more copy is needed. That's the pattern.

Have you seen those long sales pages where you scroll and scroll? Now you know why they are so long. The copywriter needs that much text in order to make their argument.

They may have thirty different beliefs they need to instill, and that takes time. It takes a lot of words. I can't tell you how many of those sales pages I've critiqued where I've told the person, "Nope, I'm not convinced. You need to write more."

That's why we see test after test proving those long sales pages outperform short ones.

(If those long sales pages are well written, that is. Many people make their sales pages long because they think that's what they are supposed to do without realizing the underlying strategy of Belief Building and claim/proof.)

You must ask: What am I selling? Commodity eggs or fancy eggs?

Ninety-nine percent of people reading this book are selling fancy eggs, and I bet that includes you. You're likely selling a product or service that requires some explaining.

The problem is, in my experience, too many smart people are selling fancy eggs but marketing them like commodity eggs.

Let's go back to the list of products at the start of this chapter. If you're selling a more complex product like a coaching program, consulting, online course, or services, your prospect feels that same resistance you felt when you went from those household items to the coaching program.

Yet, people sell these more complex products as if they're selling hand soap. When I come across Facebook ads selling $3,000 workshops with a red slash through the price and rewritten as $99, it breaks my heart.

You can't copy/paste commodity egg tactics onto a fancy egg product and expect good results.

I get it, in most cases the lessons we've learned about marketing come from merchandising tactics: coupons, buy-one-get-one, loyalty points, favorable financing, etc. But now you have another tool to use instead: Belief Building.

To guide you, here is a list of factors that determine how much education and Belief Building you must do:

- **Price of the product.** The lower the price, the less Belief Building you'll need to do.
- **Length of the sales cycle.** It takes less time to sell a gallon of milk to a family than accounting software to the government.
- **Complexity of the product.** A coaching program is more complicated to use than eggs.
- **How novel the product is.** Henry Ford had to educate horse and buggy owners on his revolutionary Model T car. It took a lot of Belief Building, but it was worth it.

The graphic below shows products that require more or less Belief Building.

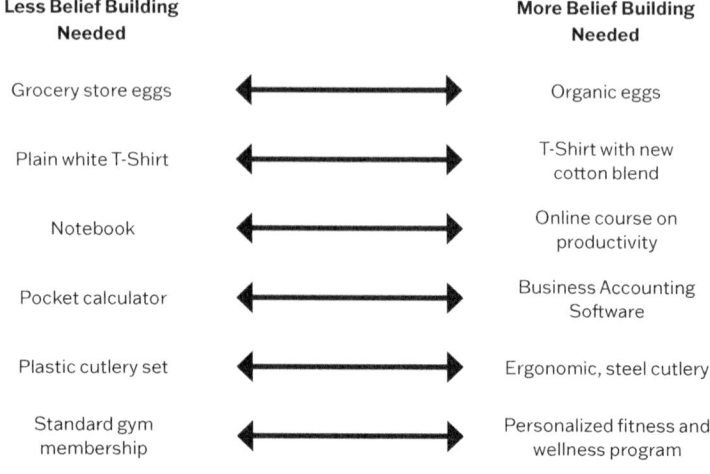

Less Belief Building Needed	More Belief Building Needed
Grocery store eggs	Organic eggs
Plain white T-Shirt	T-Shirt with new cotton blend
Notebook	Online course on productivity
Pocket calculator	Business Accounting Software
Plastic cutlery set	Ergonomic, steel cutlery
Standard gym membership	Personalized fitness and wellness program

Ask yourself, "When I scan the products on the left versus those on the right, what's the difference?"

Additionally, here are a couple of exercises to help you understand this relationship of product complexity to messaging needed:

1. **Same Product, Two Audiences:** Choose a product or service you wish to sell. Imagine explaining it to two different audiences: one that is already familiar with such a product and another that has no prior knowledge or beliefs about it. How would your explanation and selling points differ between the two audiences?

2. **From Basic to Premium:** Pick a common household commodity like dishwashing detergent. Imagine that a new, premium version of this product has been developed. Craft messages that could be used in marketing this premium product, focusing on building beliefs about its unique qualities or benefits.

Unless you're Walmart, you always want to be in a position where you *need* to build belief. Otherwise, you'll be in a race to the bottom, price-wise.

When a customer is fully aware of your product and doesn't see any difference between you and your competitors, their only choice is to buy based on price. If your product is different from others, you're able to charge higher prices. You're selling fancy eggs instead of commodity eggs.

Yes, you'll need to educate your customers on those differences, but you're now armed with the tools to do so. Now that you see the pattern and know the strategy, let's talk about your next steps.

CHAPTER TWELVE

Smart Next Steps

By BILLY BROAS

Unlike most marketing books, this book is not overly prescriptive. When we scanned the bookshelves, we saw them filled with rigid formulas and blueprints that promise success due to strict adherence to a set of magic rules.

All those other marketing books say, "Do this, do that, put this ad here."

While those books have their place, we saw a gap. We wanted to write a book that went bottom-up, not top-down. This Belief Building process isn't easy. We don't tell you exactly what to do, because we can't. You still have to do the work of learning about your customers, their beliefs, what beliefs are missing, and how you'll deploy all this through your marketing efforts.

At least now you know what is most important: understanding people, what they need, and how to genuinely connect with them.

You're no doubt eager to put this approach into practice, so to help you move ahead, we've given you six actionable steps.

Action Step #1: Revisit your current audience.
Now is a good time to go back to basics and ask the question, "Who is my customer?"

Revisit who you have been speaking to and ask yourself:

- What does my customer already know?
- How long is their chain of beliefs?
- Is this who I want to target going forward?

In teaching Belief Building, some business owners will rethink who they are targeting. In some cases, they realize they've been trying to sell a too-advanced product to beginners. In other cases, they realize they've been selling an introductory product to advanced consumers.

In both cases, the business owners made changes in their messaging, channels, testimonials, and the other areas they needed to bring into alignment in order to target their newly unveiled target customer.

Action Step #2: Complete your core messaging document.
After getting clear on your ideal customer, it's now time to do your Belief Building exercises. You can use the core messaging template we've created for you. Download it at: simplemarketingbook.com/bonus

What if all future presentations you gave incorporated Belief Building? What if you used the claim/proof model to write your next sales page?

Tiago's company uses a version of this document as the guiding light for all the content they produce.

Action Step #3: Create new marketing material.
The perfect time to read this book is before an upcoming marketing push. Do you have an upcoming product launch, website design, rebrand, newsletter rollout, or other effort where it's important to nail it?

Incorporate Belief Building, and you'll boost the persuasive power of that marketing material.

Action Step #4: Find more opportunities to incorporate Belief Building.
In addition to increasing sales of a product or service, you can use Belief Building in many ways.

Here are some ideas:

1. If you're a service provider, create a free online course that prepares prospects for your high-end services. If you find yourself always repeating the same basic information, this could take a lot of that work off your plate.
2. Launch a new product to existing customers. Educate your customers, using Belief Building, on what they need to know in order to buy this product. Then launch it, and watch them eagerly buy.
3. Use Belief Building while delivering your product. What if a teacher used Belief Building in their classroom? What if a physical therapist used it to increase compliance with their treatment plan? What if an executive coach used it to get their CEO-client to follow their advice?

When you have someone's best interest at heart and need to get them to take action, the strategies in this book are your best tool.

Action Step #5: Make the most of other trainings you've taken.

Have you invested in marketing training in the past? Are there online courses sitting in your downloads folder right now for running Facebook ads, building sales funnels, and crushing it with YouTube?

Thanks to Belief Building, what you learned in those courses can now reach its full potential. Remember, your core message is upstream—a higher-leverage activity than all that advice about marketing channels and tactics—and using it will create more cohesion and success downstream.

To make sure you put *Simple Marketing for Smart People* into action, do this short exercise:

1. Take out a pen and paper.
2. Pick the action from the five I've listed above that you're most excited to implement. Write it in your notes.
3. Finally, write down when you will devote at least thirty minutes to this. Write down where it will be, who will be involved, and what you'll need to have success in that work session.

We hope this book taught you a lot, but ultimately, we hope it gets you to take decisive, purposeful action. If you do, we know you'll see big success.

CHAPTER THIRTEEN

A Final Word of Advice for Smart Marketers

By BILLY BROAS

It was 2011, and one of my email subscribers, Nick, clicked a sales email promoting my beer brewing course. This was after having received a series of emails that educated him on my approach and made an argument for my brewing philosophy.

He clicked the link in the email, read my sales page, and purchased my online course.

Nick dove into the course material and loved it. He started brewing weekly batches of beer and got pretty good.

Then, his local Ohio brewery announced a competition. In the competition, home brewers would enter their best beer and the winner would get to brew their beer at the brewery and serve it to the brewery's customers.

Nick was still a beginner and questioned his skills, but he entered the competition anyway.

He brewed a German beer recipe that I taught in my online course—but added his own twist. His creation blew away the judges, and they awarded him first place. Nick couldn't believe it—he'd won. But the good news didn't end there. The brewery was so impressed that they offered Nick a job as an assistant brewer, which he took.

It was a dream come true. Nick disliked his current job, and while at work, he'd often dream about working at a brewery. So, he ditched his old job and took the offer to become a professional brewer.

He thrived, and the town took notice. Eventually, a brewery down the road had a job opening for the head brewer position, which they offered to Nick. He happily accepted.

From a lousy job to head brewer—talk about a happy ending.

I'm sure glad I sent that promotional email.

Who knows if Nick would have still wound up becoming a head brewer. Probably, but you never know.

My point is this: stop being so quiet.

Stop being afraid to publish your thoughts. I totally get that you're overwhelmed by marketing. I know it's frustrating to try and compete with the viral videos, the clickbait, and the flashy influencers.

The internet often doesn't feel like a place where a smart person can be heard.

Rest assured, people want to hear from you. You don't need to dance in videos or use gimmicks or become a flashy influencer to get your message across.

So many consumers are tired of that noise and BS and simply want someone to speak to them like an adult.

You're in the perfect position to help them, too. You have all the necessary traits. You care about your clients, you're skilled at your craft, and you're a problem-solver.

Give voice to your experience. Educate your prospects. Help them make the right decisions along their journey.

Show why you've created your solution and how it works. Show your prospects how it benefits them. Show who it's perfect for. Show who your solution *isn't* designed for.

Be emotionally unattached to the sale. Instead, focus on educating. When you clear up your prospect's misconceptions, lay all possible paths on the table, and make an argument for your recommended path, the sales will come naturally.

Do your job with Belief Building, and let the chips fall where they fall.

Belief Building reveals the truth. It confronts all assumptions, speaks to all the elephants in the room, and backs up claims with proof.

Rather than relying on hype, exaggeration, and deception, Belief Building cuts through those smokescreens and lets your product's truth shine through.

If you believe in your product, you have nothing to worry about.

Smart people who go into business for themselves need to do a better job of talking about what they do. We hate to see all the smart people out there with excellent products and services who aren't giving those solutions adequate voice. We worry about all the customers getting ripped off by companies and gurus with flashy marketing tactics, but not much else.

Now, you no longer have to sit on the sideline. You have your missing manual. You know how to cut through the noise by being smarter, not louder.

To conclude this book, we'd like to leave you with a few dos and don'ts.

Don't get caught up building a complex, confusing, always-breaking NASA brewery with your marketing. There will always be another shiny object. You don't need them. All you need is knowledge of your prospect, knowledge of your product, and the Belief Building approach.

Don't obsess over channels and tactics. Whenever a guru tells you, "You MUST be on XYZ platform," ignore them. There are endless ways to reach your prospect; what matters most is your message.

Don't fall for the false choice between making money and selling your soul. You can make money and do it ethically. Follow the golden rule of marketing—market to others as you want to be marketed to—and you'll keep your morals intact.

Do treat marketing as education. Know that an educated prospect is a better prospect. Dishonest marketers prefer to keep their prospects in the dark. That's not us.

Do entertain as you educate. Education isn't supposed to be boring. The best way to get your point across is to make it enjoyable for your reader.

Do realize your knowledge and experience can benefit others.

Marketing can be fun, creative, powerful, honest, human, intellectual, and classy. And most importantly—simple.

Rooting for you,
Billy and Tiago

Acknowledgments

Thank you to my loving wife, Laura. You're always there for me no matter what, and I'm a lucky husband. And thanks to my kids, Ana and William, who never fail to make me laugh. I'm a lucky dad, too.

Thank you to our book coach, Isabella Masucci. You guided me through unfamiliar terrain, and it's doubtful I or this book would have emerged without your experience, skill, and kindness.

Thank you to Tiago Forte. You and I have had many fun adventures, but producing a book together may be the best yet. Thank you for your support and desire to get this information into the hands of those who need it.

Thank you to Kristina Haahr, our editor, who made this book sing with a clear voice. And Maya Lim, our branding pro, who designed a beautiful (and smart) book cover.

Finally, thanks to all my clients, students, newsletter subscribers, and anyone who has trusted me and put my material into practice in their business. I'm rooting for you.

Billy Broas

About the Authors

Billy Broas has a gift for making the complex simple, a skill that's helpful when it comes to creating a marketing message. As a messaging strategist, consultant, and educator, Billy has helped hundreds of businesses convey their value in a more compelling way.

Billy is the creator of the popular Five Lightbulbs® messaging framework, which makes it easy to implement the principles shared inside Simple Marketing for Smart People.

Billy, his wife, and their two young children live in San Diego, where they enjoy warm weather, hikes, and delicious Mexican food.

BillyBroas.com
FiveLightbulbs.com

Tiago Forte is recognized as a leading authority on productivity, teaching professionals worldwide how technology can elevate their effectiveness and creativity.

His book, *Building a Second Brain*, has sold over 200,000 copies and pioneered the field of personal knowledge management.

Previously, Tiago's diverse experiences included working in microfinance in Latin America, Peace Corps service in Ukraine, and consulting on product development in San Francisco. He currently resides in Long Beach, California, with his wife Lauren and their two children.

Buildingasecondbrain.com

Printed in Great Britain
by Amazon

44612121R00086